DESIGN FOR CROSS-CULTURAL LEARNING

Mildred Sikkema

Agnes Niyekawa

Intercultural Press, Inc.

Yarmouth, Maine

c

Some of the material in this book is drawn from an earlier work by the authors, *Cross-cultural Learning and Self-Growth*, and is used herein with the permission of the International Association of Schools of Social Work.

For information, address Intercultural Press, P.O. Box 768, Yarmouth, Maine 04096

Library of Congress Catalogue Card Number 86-081361

Library of Congress Cataloging-in-Publication Data

Sikkema, Mildred.
    Design for cross-cultural learning.

    Bibliography: p.
    Includes index.
    1. Intercultural education.   2. Intercultural communication. I. Niyekawa, Agnes. II. Title.
LC1099.S543   1987   370.19'6   86-81361
ISBN 0-933662-63-7

Printed in the United States of America

CONTENTS

To the students and to the people in the communities in

which the students lived,

for their contribution to the development of the field of

cross-cultural learning.

1 INTRODUCTION

Education is the acquisition of the art of the utilization of knowledge . . .
Theoretical ideas should always find important applications within the
pupil's curriculum.
Alfred N. Whitehead, *The Aims of Education and Other Essays*, 1950

This book addresses the need to educate students to be more effective in dealing with people from different cultural backgrounds. It proposes a design for cross-cultural learning that can be applied anywhere in the educational process from high school through graduate and professional training, or, indeed, in cross-cultural training for adults outside formal educational contexts. The design is based on the experience of the authors in conducting experimental programs for American and Hong Kong Chinese social work students, including field placements in Guam, the Philippines, Hong Kong, and Hawaii.

It is intended to meet the needs of people at all levels of society to understand the meaning and significance of cultural differences and to provide educators with a tool for enabling students to achieve an active rather than passive understanding of those differences.

Today, in this rapidly shrinking world, many of us find ourselves unexpectedly acquiring, say, an Iranian brother-in-law or a Vietnamese daughter-in-law. People from countries occupying an obscure place on our mental maps suddenly appear in the flesh and we experience our first real intercultural encounter. Interacting with a person from another culture in a face-to-face situation, where understanding and being understood are

1

essential, is quite different from observing such a person from a comfortable distance. Such encounters are, however, becoming more and more common in today's world.

Despite the large number of individuals who come in contact with people of other ethnic and national backgrounds, the number who can interact with them without misunderstandings is disproportionately small. Many consider themselves competent in dealing with "foreigners" without realizing how little they understand what they are doing.

A professional with years of teaching experience abroad once said, "When I advise a foreign student who has just arrived, I test his English by telling him a joke. If he doesn't laugh, I know he needs English classes before he can enroll in any of the regular academic courses." He did not seem to realize that understanding an American joke requires familiarity with American culture as well as language, nor did he take into account the fact that people of different cultures may not laugh at the same things. What people from one culture consider funny may be perceived by people of another culture or subculture as poor taste.

We assume that people of another culture or subculture see, feel, and think as we do. It is true that certain basic emotions, such as joy and sorrow, are common to all cultures, but the ways of expressing these feelings may not be the same. Much misunderstanding is caused by the assumption that our own reactions are universal.

ACTIVE *VS.* PASSIVE UNDERSTANDING

The reason for the surprising lack of awareness of the need for deeper cross-cultural understanding may be that the majority of well-educated people have a "passive" understanding of other cultures and subcultures that gives them the feeling that they know the other cultures. Traveling to many foreign countries, meeting and interacting with foreign representatives at conferences and banquets, and having a few acquaintances from other countries or other ethnic groups are, however, no guarantee that a person can function well in intercultural settings.

Literary translations and foreign movies reveal a great deal of commonality across cultures. Themes of love, conflict, suffering, and happiness can be shared, and one has no problem in identifying with heroes and heroines, even though they are dressed in different clothes and are speaking different languages. Actually, the ease with which we understand the characters, no matter how alien the setting, adds to a false sense of knowing and understanding.

We have been speaking thus far of "passive" understanding; however, when people of different cultures or subcultures interact in face-to-face situations in which egos are involved, another kind of understanding is required—"active" understanding. Passive understanding can be attained without ever leaving one's home town. It can be achieved to a significant extent by studying the literature, philosophy, religion, history, or art of a particular culture. At a time when international cooperation is essential for survival, learning to see people of other cultures as more similar to us than different is essential. The efforts of those who work for this type of intercultural education must be appreciated. But for those who will be interacting with people of other cultures, particularly on their own home ground or in situations typically encountered in professions where more than superficial communication is required, such passive understanding is far from sufficient.

A familiar experience will illustrate the difference between passive and active understanding. Many of us have developed special attachments and identifications with particular groups of people through their literature, history, or art. Casual contacts with a high school or college classmate from Argentina may stimulate a strong interest in that country. Learning French or German in high school may have a similar effect. The romantic love and admiration we may have developed for an exotic culture and people may evaporate, however, when we eventually come into substantive contact with those people. An innocent, well-intentioned comment or action may provoke a totally unexpected reaction. In certain cultures, for instance, asking a man about the health of his mother or sister is tantamount to accusing him of intimate knowledge of her and may lead to an extremely hostile response, embarrassment, and/or hurt feelings, even to the breaking off of the relationship.

Such a minor and, to you, completely normal thing as a joke intended to relax tension may be taken as an insult. You behave in a way acceptable in your own culture; you are eager to make friends with these new people but they begin to withdraw and you do not know why. You may attempt to explain that you meant no harm; you may apologize and ask what you did that was wrong, but even that may not restore the relationship. In one instance, an American girl cleaned the room while her Thai roommate was having breakfast in the dormitory dining hall. When the roommate returned, she became upset, cried, and left the room. Later it became clear that the American girl had placed the Thai girl's skirt on the pillow portion of the bed. In the Thai culture, the head is sacred and putting a piece of clothing associated with a lesser part of the body on a place reserved for the head was one of the worst possible insults. Friends and advisors tried to explain to the Thai girl that the American girl's intentions were only good, but the involuntary reaction was so deep that she refused to room with the

American girl again. It is hardly necessary to point out that the situation could have happened in reverse; the Thai girl's best intentions might have offended the American girl's sensibilities.

The essential difference between passive and active understanding lies in intellectual and rational understanding on the one hand and affective or emotional understanding on the other. It is much easier to understand and accept cultural differences at the rational level than at the emotional level where reactions are not usually under conscious control.

Most of us have gone through the experience of being convinced at the rational level that the foreign food our host is serving should be tried, yet at the emotional level experience feelings of such anxiety and discomfort that it shows in physical reactions to the food. It may be just a frown or an intonation, or it may extend to such bodily reactions as restlessness, constipation, or a vomit reflex. It is this type of reaction that is relevant to active understanding; it is at this level that the ego is involved.

Active understanding requires the development at gut level of an attitude of acceptance, respect, and tolerance of cultural differences. This can hardly be accomplished through traditional classroom methods, because learning in the classroom takes place primarily at the intellectual level. Descriptions and analyses of other cultures and peoples may be presented, but the student does not experience the embarrassment of making mistakes or the joy of successfully functioning in another culture. In other words, in the classroom there is relatively little involvement at the emotional level with the culture under study.

Leading educators have pointed out that more than the conventional college education is required to develop this type of understanding. Harris Wofford, formerly associate director of the Peace Corps and president of Bryn Mawr College, says:

> The gap in understanding among nations and peoples, if not widening, is still enormous. The inadequacy of conventional academic education to close this gap—to prepare the people here and elsewhere for citizenship in the twentieth-century world community—is becoming obvious.[1]

How, then, is active understanding to be attained? Wofford points to the Peace Corp's form of "experiential" education—learning by doing on a world scale—as a possible way of filling this gap. In discussing experiential education, Wofford states:

> The division between teacher and student is blurred because the definition of a good Peace Corps Volunteer includes the possession of the spirit

---

[1]Wofford, 1960, p 136.

of learning. If the Volunteer does not have the learning spirit, that fact is going to be discovered in the difficult assignment in which he is engaged. People are going to sense that he has come to do good against them. In the Peace Corps you have to learn from those you teach, you have to learn by doing, and it is not only learning by doing, but learning by going. Migration, people on the move, going into a radically new setting, with the possibility of trading the old life for a new one—this is part of the energy and motivation in the Peace Corps kind of education, just as it was for those who migrated to Israel or, in earlier days, to America.[2]

It is through this type of experiential learning—learning to live in a different physical environment under a different set of cultural values— that active understanding takes place. Most important, we become acutely aware of our own cultural values and learn to take nothing for granted.

THE CULTURAL FRAMEWORK

The reason it is so important in intercultural situations to be aware of our dependence on our own culture and the structural framework that it provides is precisely because these things are taken so much for granted. We are aware of knowing the things we have been taught, but what we have learned through experience, without conscious awareness, tends to escape our notice. For example, as we encounter people of our own culture we are constantly making judgments, often non-consciously,[3] as to age, race, occupation, social status and educational background, using as a basis for these judgments physical appearance, dress, speech, and behavior. The cues we use to make these decisions are usually so subtle that it is difficult to explain how and why we reached a particular conclusion. Yet, these cues help us predict another person's behavior to some extent, and our initial conversation is made easier. Using the same cues with someone from another culture, however, may not work. Americans frequently underestimate the age of Japanese, judging a college student in her midtwenties to be a girl of 14 or 15, or assuming a forty-year-old man to be fresh out of college. Since one constantly adjusts one's speech and behavior accordingly, underestimating a person's age can result in insulting him. All

---

[2]Wofford, as quoted in Taylor, 1969, p 110.

[3]In this context, and from time to time elsewhere in the book, the authors use the word "non-conscious" to refer to basic human mental and emotional processes that are out-of-awareness. Their intent is to avoid some of the more complex connotations of the words "subconscious" and "unconscious."

too often we unconsciously treat the newly arrived foreign student who has difficulty expressing himself in English as if he were a child. In other words, we judge him as we would an American who spoke English in the same imperfect way.

Obviously, then, cues that help us function effectively in our own culture may be misleading in a cross-cultural situation. This is true of every aspect of behavior. Within our own culture we develop a sensitivity to others as to what is likely to make a person angry, what his facial expressions mean, what things he considers too personal for discussion, whether his words are to be interpreted literally or have a more subtle meaning behind them. It is impossible to function in any society without having certain expectations as to the behavior of others. We are, then, understandably unsettled by someone whose behavior we cannot predict, such as a drunken or mentally ill person.

In intercultural situations we are likely to have the same reactions of anxiety or even fear when customary cues fail to predict the behavior of others. Until we learn the cues of the other culture, we find ourselves in an unstructured situation, not knowing what to do or what to expect. This unsettling experience is called "culture shock."

Culture shock is the state of disorientation experienced by a person entering a new culture or subculture as he discovers for the first time that many of the things to which he is accustomed are unique to his own culture. The more culture-bound he is, the greater the shock. A monocultural person may be likened to the fish that knows the difference between comfortable and uncomfortable waters but does not realize its dependence on its aquatic surroundings until removed from them. The monocultural person is aware of those aspects of his culture that have been pointed out to him as being unique to it, but is unaware of the vast portion of his culture that he has learned unconsciously in the process of growing up.

A monocultural American couple travels to Japan for a vacation. They decide to stay at a traditional Japanese inn rather than at a Western-style hotel. They find that their room opens onto a Japanese garden with a waterfall, and they are glad they chose the inn. The husband starts to take off his travel suit and, without knocking, the maid enters, bringing towels and tea. He is embarrassed, turns his back, and continues changing his clothes. The maid helps him, which embarrasses him all the more. When she finally disappears, he sits down with his wife to have some tea. After tea the wife starts to take off her stockings in order to put on Japanese footgear. The maid reappears to announce that the bath is ready. They find the maid is also present throughout the dinner to serve them and still later to make their bed. By the time they get to bed they have had enough of the maid's interruptions and wish she would not appear unless called. They also find it disturbing that the sliding doors to their room cannot be locked. They cannot understand why Japanese inns are so highly recommended. What they do not realize is the degree to which they, as Americans, have come to value privacy. To a Japanese, personal attention and service, including having one's back scrubbed in the bath, are essential for relaxation, while lack of privacy, to an American, interferes with relaxation.

During a short vacation, an isolated incident such as this may remain just that for the travelers. However, a series of such incidents might shake them out of the comfortable cocoon of their own culture and make them aware for the first time that some of the values, such as privacy, personal freedom and personal ownership, that they assume are shared by all people of the world, are actually peculiar to their own culture. Also, they learn that the cues that they have been using to predict other people's behavior are culture-based. In learning the ways of the new culture, they must unlearn some of their own ways.

In other words, the first step toward understanding another culture is becoming aware of one's own cultural habits and values so that they will not interfere with learning those of the new culture. Once this step is taken, learning a third and fourth culture will be easier. This is why a person who has achieved an active understanding of a second culture through experiential learning is aware of the relativity of cultural values and develops at a visceral level an attitude of acceptance, respect, and tolerance toward other cultures.

BASIC PREMISES

The major aim of this educational design is to prepare students to function effectively in any culture or subculture and to help them grow toward becoming more flexible and creative through experiential learning. To accomplish this goal, it is important that the active understanding gained in one culture be easily transferable to other cultures, that is, capable of generalization. It is believed that students, by being given minimum culture-specific instruction and training, will search and find out for themselves such things as customs in greeting, or in accepting or declining invitations, ways of interacting with people of different social positions, and so on. The students are expected to sort out their observations on their own and determine which are recurrent cultural behavior patterns and which can be dismissed as idiosyncratic personal characteristics. This puts the students in the role of full-time learners.

The lack of structure in the learning situation forces the student to face ambiguity and gradually to build a structure that will serve as a framework for learning. The exercise of trying various alternatives until the most suitable or workable solution is found—whether in interpreting some aspect of the culture or in building a general framework of understanding—is considered an important part of the training. By going through such an experience once, a student will get an idea of how to do it again the next time. In other words, he learns "how to learn" another culture. He will develop, it is hoped, an aptness for sensing or perceiving another person's feelings, views and needs, regardless of the cultural background.

It is also believed that this exercise in building sensible patterns out of initial ambiguities will move the student not only toward biculturality but also in the direction of multiculturality. The emphasis placed on the process of learning another culture rather than on its content is designed to help the student develop a sensitivity to cues in any culture with which he comes in contact. This is one of the most significant objectives of the design.

The built-in ambiguity is also intended to force the student to engage in divergent thinking. Just as he learns much about his own culture by stepping outside of it and viewing it objectively, so does he discover more about himself. He may discover strengths heretofore dormant, such as a readiness to risk himself in uncertain environments, an ability to look beyond the known to discover different and perhaps untried approaches in challenging situations, or an assurance of his ability to deal with a variety of unpredictable events. Except in the rare instance where the experience poses a threat to the total personality—the likelihood of which is reduced by the provision of certain supports—the student returns to his own culture a new person, with much more confidence in himself.

This design for cross-cultural learning is based on the assumption that the above goals are achievable within the limitations of a well-planned curriculum. The authors believe it is a feasible program for most educational institutions to implement, given a modicum of institutional and faculty support and flexibility and a commitment to the ultimate goal.

It is imperative that we find the means of establishing effective communication among people of different cultures and that opportunities be made available to students to gain a more comprehensive and realistic cultural understanding of themselves and others. Asa Hilliard states the challenge in terms of a broad educational goal when he writes:

> . . . every school subject if taught truthfully and realistically requires a
> plural cultural perspective. Science, literature, the behavioral sciences

. . . all must be freed from the monocultural ethnocentric focus that characterizes most standard course work . . .[4]

The program described in this book offers one approach to meeting that challenge.

---

[4]Quoted in Wasilewski and Seelye, 1979, 64.

DESIGN FOR CROSS-CULTURAL LEARNING

2

Cross-cultural learning as we use the term here has been succinctly described by David Hoopes as "a tool for adapting to change, to a world in which pluralism and the need to function effectively in different cultural environments will become increasingly important for an increasing number of people."[5]

Since one can expect educational programs to be effective only if they rest on sound theoretical foundations, we will begin by discussing the conceptual framework for cross-cultural learning.

THEORETICAL FOUNDATIONS

Convergent and Divergent Thinking

In the previous chapter it was proposed that becoming aware of our own culture is the first step in understanding another. However, it is difficult to develp a clear awareness of our own culture because we take so much for granted. We are provided by society with a culturally established framework in which to operate and predict the behavior of other people. Our judgments and behavior become almost automatic. For instance, we have different sets of expectations as to appropriate dress and behavior in different structured social situations such as meetings, luncheons, picnics, cock-

---

[5]Personal communication, April, 1983.

tail parties, dinner parties, wedding receptions, or funerals. We alter our behavior depending on what is expected of us. When we find ourselves in a completely new situation and do not know how we are supposed to behave, we feel uncomfortable. We experience anxiety because the situation is ambiguous; we do not know what the rules are. We all have had such experiences in the process of growing up—the first date, the first formal banquet, the first meeting with an important person, the first foreign meal served without knives and forks.

All other things being equal, people tend to avoid an ambiguous situation in favor of a structured one. Abraham Maslow points out that each of us is subject to two sets of forces: one which leans toward defense or safety, the other toward growth.[6] In Maslow's terms, it is the force of safety that makes one choose the familiar over the unfamiliar. Related to Maslow's two forces are two basic cognitive modes identified by Guilford[7] in his factor-analytic study of the intellect, namely, convergent and divergent modes of thinking.

Convergent thinking refers essentially to logical thinking, with a number of facts leading to one conclusion. In contrast, divergent thinking, using a fact or stimulus as a starting point, can go in different directions. There is no one correct answer in divergent thinking; a number of alternatives are available. Getzels and Jackson contrast the two modes of thinking as follows: "The convergent mode tends toward retaining the known, learning the predetermined, and conserving what is," while the divergent mode "tends toward revising the known, exploring the undetermined, and constructing what might be."[8]

Although both processes are found in all individuals, they are found in varying proportions. A person for whom the convergent mode is primary tends toward the usual and expected, while a person for whom the divergent mode is primary tends toward the novel and speculative. Put in other terms, one mode represents intellectual acquisitiveness and conformity; the other, intellectual inventiveness and innovation. To engage in divergent thinking, one must be willing to risk oneself, to take chances and be prepared for unexpected, possibly negative, outcomes.

Edward Hall, in his perceptive book, *Beyond Culture*,[9] identifies the problem as a lack of holistic vision.

> . . . Western man has created chaos by denying that part of his self that integrates while enshrining the parts that fragment experience. . . .

[6]Maslow, 1956, 37–38.
[7]Guilford, 1959.
[8]Getzels and Jackson, 1962, 13–14.
[9]Hall, 1976, #7, 173–4.

Western man uses only a small fraction of his mental capacities; there are many different and legitimate ways of thinking; we in the West value one of these ways above all others—the one we call 'logic', a linear system that has been with us since Socrates. . . . We have been taught to think linearly rather than comprehensively, . . . Given our linear, step-by-step, compartmentalized way of thinking, fostered by the schools and public media, it is impossible for our leaders to consider events comprehensively. . . .

Hall continues:

If the young can do well what many schools require, the mind that results from this process is one with little experience in creative thinking and solving real-life problems. . . . Without stating it in so many words, American education assumes a brain that compartmentalizes and localizes knowledge, a stimulus-response organ in which a single stimulus leads to a uniform response. Certainly, this is the way everything is taught. Yet, according to Luria, the brain functions in several different ways. Some functions . . . are integrative in character.

For Hall, linear is comparable to convergent thinking and comprehensive (or non-linear) to divergent thinking.

Robert Ornstein, who has been involved for a long time in studying the functioning of the two sides of the brain, refers, when examining this issue, to

'two modes of consciousness,' the logical and the intuitive. The logical mode of knowledge operates sequentially, arriving at a truth inferentially, proceeding logically from one element to another. Intuition operates simultaneously, is concerned with the sets of relations among elements, which receive their meaning from the overall holistic content. . . . Reason, then, primarily involves an analysis of discrete elements, inferentially (sequentially) linked; intuition involves simultaneous perception of the whole.[10]

He proposes two complementary principles in human thought:

. . . an ordered sequencer which underlies language and 'rational' mentation, and a simultaneous processor . . . intuition, a faculty of holistic perception. The perception of the holistic aspects of reality demands . . . a simultaneous mode of experience.[11]

---

[10]Ornstein, 1976. 26.
[11]Ornstein, 1976, 30.

Analytical, rational, sequential (convergent) thinking is associated primarily with the left brain hemisphere, while integrative, intuitive, simultaneous (divergent) thinking is associated with the right hemisphere.[12] Regretting that our educational system generally fosters only analytical, sequential, convergent thinking (the functions of the left brain), Ornstein, Hall, and others make a strong case for inclusion of opportunities for students to develop the integrative, intuitive, divergent ways of thinking associated with right brain functioning. One way to develop this kind of thinking and the simultaneity of perception involved in it is through focused field experience designed to engage students in learning at the affective level in real life situations. Actually, many leading educators, recognizing its educational power, are committed to the inclusion of focused experiential learning in academic programs, but most have shunned it as being unworthy of academic credit. But this is the crux of the matter—experiential learning properly planned and related to an appropriate cognitive framework is just as credit worthy as normal classroom (analytical, linear, convergent) learning, and both are essential ingredients to a sound educational program.

Affective Learning

In a story drawn from his own experience, John Wallace,[13] of the School for International Training, illustrates strikingly the interplay between intellectual knowledge and experience. As a college student he had written a term paper on the impact of drought on the economy of certain countries. He passed the course but doing the paper had no significant effect on him; he had not changed in any way. Twenty years later, standing on a street in Calcutta, he saw the bodies of people dead from starvation being carted away, victims of drought and famine—"the facts of my under-graduate paper had turned into funeral pyres." The "intellectual awareness" became "emotional awareness"—and, Wallace says, "I changed." His work interests changed as did his views about people; indeed, his life changed. Experience had connected with the intellectual knowledge, each giving meaning to the other and creating the conditions for change and growth in the person.

The point is that if we are going to provide educational experiences that result in holistic perceptions of the global village in which we live, we need

---

[12]This is not to imply rigid separation between the functioning of the right and left hemispheres of the brain. Recent studies in neuroscience, while confirming hemispheric differences, point out that in any activity different parts of the brain are involved (*Newsweek*, February 7, 1983).
[13]Wallace, 1977, 23–24.

to develop curricula that combine the cognitive with the affective.

In discussing the need for affective learning in cross-cultural education, Hoopes notes that the "unconscious nature" of our "deeply rooted and culturally conditioned perceptions of reality," from which our communication styles and behavior patterns derive, makes them relatively inaccessible and resistant to change. Becoming aware of these perceptions, he continues, is "an emotional event derived from experience [as Wallace says] rather than an idea attained through an intellectual process." And he adds, "If we are going to come to grips with the concept of cultural relativity and take significant steps toward cultural self-awareness, we have to become fully engaged with our own perceptions, our own behaviors, and our own communication patterns."[14]

Harold Taylor, in his seminal book, *The World as Teacher*, puts it this way:

> Through the normal course of growing up in his own culture, each child is taught what he is intended to know, and his sense of identity, his attitudes, depend on the cultural milieu in which they are developed and what he has been taught to believe about himself. In order to know anything, it is necessary to be able to relate it to something already known, to look at the world from one's own point of view. But to do that means narrowing the world to a single perspective, thus distorting the reality of what can only be seen clearly and truthfully from a larger view and from many perspectives.[15]

Selective Perception

The child's "knowing" is accomplished through perceptual learning within the framework of a culturally established perceptual system. The process of perceptual learning is described by Gibson, an authority on perception, as one of learning "what to attend to, both overtly and covertly." It involves learning to detect the critical or distinctive features of objects and events and to abstract the general properties. Although Gibson focuses his work on the perception of physical dimensions and does not concern himself with social perception, one can infer from many of his statements that there are differential effects on perceptual learning due to cultural differences. He states that "the education of the perceptual system depends mainly on the individual's history of exposure to the environment."[16]

---

[14]Hoopes, 1979, 16–17.
[15]Taylor, 1969, 1–2.
[16]Gibson, 1966, 268.

Gibson also discusses the acquisition of "what might be called economical perception," which he defines as "the ability to avoid distraction—to concentrate on one thing at a time in the face of everything going on in the environment—and yet to accomplish as much knowing as possible." Thus, "only the information required to identify a thing economically tends to be picked up from a complex of stimulus information. All the other available information that would be required to specify its unique and complete identity in the whole universe of things is not attended to."[17]

In other words, perception is selective. In the process of growing up in a culture, the child learns to focus on those attributes important for obtaining essential information in his environment and to screen out the rest. What is attended to in Gibson's terms are the critical or distinctive features or "criterial attributes" in the theories of Jerome Bruner and others.[18]

It is not hard to see how cultural differences can lead to misunderstanding because of selective attention to different aspects of behavior or different inferences drawn from the same behavior. For instance, we have learned from experience how to estimate a person's age. Although we may not be able to identify all the cues, we do use them in estimating age. When we meet someone of a different race, we frequently find that the cues or criterial attributes we are accustomed to using do not work, and we end up underestimating or overestimating the person's age, which suggests that criterial attributes vary from culture to culture. We have learned to attend selectively to our own criterial attributes and at the same time to screen out the criterial attributes used in the other culture to differentiate between twenty- and forty-year-olds.

Language, as well as behavior, also plays a role in determining the criterial attributes for selective perception. There are a number of studies on how the vocabulary, syntax, or phonology of a language influence the perception of those who speak it.[19]

Language provides readily available labels for perceptual categorization. All items referred to by the same label have certain attributes in common. One learns to attend selectively to those attributes in using that particular label. For instance, one concept frequently used in Japan in relation to art and individual taste is *shibui*. There is no equivalent term in English, so the concept cannot be easily explained. It has been described as "beauty that is understated, never obvious, deceptively simple while really being complex." This, however, is not sufficient information to enable a non-Japa-

---

[17]Gibson, 286.
[18]Bruner, Goodnow, and Austin, 1956; Brown, 1958.
[19]For a more detailed discussion of attribution theory, see Triandis in Brislin, 1975.

nese to classify an object as being beautiful in a *shibui* way. One has to be exposed to a number of items classified as shibui to grasp what the criterial attributes are. Yet the Japanese child will learn this concept with little conscious effort, just as he learns all other concepts of his culture. As the American must struggle to learn the concept of shibui, so must the Japanese struggle to learn the meaning of "I'm sorry." The word "sorry" is used on a number of different occasions with a common element, but it is hard for a Japanese to see the common element when these same occasions require distinctly different expressions in Japanese. He is likely to consider the expression an apology and to become confused when he tells an American friend of his father's death and the friend replies "I'm sorry."

These examples show the effect of geographical, cultural, and linguistic environment on non-conscious learning. Perceptual learning in these cases was not accomplished through training; it came naturally while the individual was growing up. It should be remembered that what is learned in this way gets repeatedly reinforced and that the resulting non-conscious behaviors, including the making of perceptual inferences, become automatic. The interpretation of behaviors and events is immediate and requires little thinking or conscious evaluation. These automatic habits are not easy to break, but there is little need to break them as long as they are functional in the society in which one lives. In other words, one is rewarded for convergent thinking, for "retaining the known, learning the predetermined, and conserving what is," in the normal range of functioning in society.[20]

When you step out of your own culture into a new one, however, this habit of convergent thinking tends to be broken. Through the mistakes you make in the new culture, by using habits from the old, you become aware of the cultural influences that have shaped your own patterns of thinking and behaving. Further, as a result of going through a series of ego-experiences involving both failure and success, an active—as opposed to passive—understanding of the new culture is achieved. As pointed out in the previous chapter, culture shock is an essential ingredient of learning another culture.

Culture Learning

Learning a second culture is much like learning a second language: the more similar the language, the easier it is to learn the second language; but the interference, or negative transfer, is also greater. When two cultures are similar, minor differences frequently go unnoticed and assumptions of

---

[20]Getzels and Jackson, 13–14.

similarity are made that prevent the learning of the subtle nuances of the second culture. For this reason, a culture quite different from one's own is more likely to shake one out of one's cultural habits, owing to the greater emotional and intellectual shock. Just as we maintain that culture shock is essential to the achievement of active understanding of another culture, so we also maintain that the choice of a non-Western culture as the second culture for the Western learner will have a greater overall impact.

With the realization that he can no longer use his own cultural framework, the learner is left to continue on his own, functioning in a rather uncomfortable and ambiguous situation until a new framework is provided or until he structures one himself. In this design, learning how to learn another culture is a more important goal than learning the specifics of the culture, and going through this stage of facing ambiguities is considered essential in learning how to learn. The students are not told about the values and customs in the second culture or about the behavior of the people. They are expected to find them out by groping. Putting together what at the beginning seem isolated and unrelated events, looking for consistent patterns, and eventually developing some overall structure as a framework for that culture are all exercises in the learning process. Learning to tolerate ambiguities until one knows more about the situation can have a generalizable effect, not only on learning the new culture but also on the personal development of the learner.

Since the codes of the new culture are not given, the student may try alternative ways of interpreting events and deciding how to behave. This forces him to engage in divergent thinking. Thus, learning a second culture is qualitatively different from the usual type of learning in schools. In general, advancement in education within one's own culture involves specialization. In learning the new subject matter, the student utilizes the cognitive mode developed so far and learns to make finer differentiations in what was an undifferentiated whole. In learning a second culture, however, the student must not only learn to make finer differentiations, but he must also learn to ignore the system of criterial attributes that was used in his first culture and to make differentiations along a new set of criterial attributes.

Uriel G. Foa and Martin M. Chemers[21] point out this difference in role behavior when they say that socialization involves learning to differentiate, while acculturation requires both an increase in differentiation and the forgetting of certain previously learned differentiations. High intelligence or ability in convergent thinking does not make the task any easier. What is

---

[21]Foa and Chemers, 1967, 45–57.

required is an ability in divergent thinking and a flexibility in cognitive reorganization.

Psychologists tend to agree that a non-authoritarian person who is open-minded, tolerant of ambiguity, and flexible will make a better adjustment in a new culture than the opposite type; the authoritarian personality who is closed-minded, cannot accept views different from his own, is ethnocentric and thus prejudiced against people of another ethnic background, considers his cultural values to be absolute, and would like to see those who violate these values punished. The authoritarian person is submissive toward those above him but aggressive toward those under him. He tends to dichotomize the world into black and white, and cannot tolerate grey areas. Everything must be neatly categorized. In other words, he has no tolerance for ambiguity.

Our initial involvement in a cross-cultural situation, however, is fraught with ambiguity. We do not know the codes of behavior or the cues for effective communication. A familiar structure is lacking. The result is anxiety which then serves as a motivational force to resolve the ambiguity. There is a tendency sometimes to provide a list of do's and don't's in order to reduce this anxiety. Such a list, however, prevents students from learning to understand the culture—a necessity if they are to become cross-culturally oriented. We consider learning to cope with ambiguity and experiencing the attendant culture shock to be key elements in becoming multicultural. We therefore make deliberate use of ambiguity in the design.

In an ambiguous situation—when one does not know, for instance, whether the other person is making a request or only a suggestion—the student must decide on his own how to interpret the behavior. When he misinterprets and communication fails, he has to figure out what went wrong. It is at this point that the tools of affective cross-cultural learning, provided for in this design, come most importantly into play. The best way for the student to relieve his anxiety and improve the communication is to become more fully aware of how his own culture-bound perceptions are interfering. He needs also to look for subtle, especially non-verbal, cues to the meaning of what is happening and to suspend judgment and remain tolerant of ambiguity until understanding is achieved. Out of the frustration of failure and in trying to make sense of ambiguities, he will develop new perceptions and experience satisfaction of achievement. Events which previously appeared to be isolated and unrelated will connect with each other, confusing behaviors will take on pattern and consistency, and the student will be able, slowly but surely, to start putting together a coherent picture of how the culture works.

Coping with ambiguous situations in this way means learning how to learn another culture through engaging in divergent thinking and letting the impulse toward growth win out over the desire for security. In this process the learner discovers abilities in himself, hidden heretofore, which enable him to function with greater ease and confidence in any culture. In short, he acquires cross-cultural competence.

This program for cross-cultural learning attempts to remedy the shortcomings of a curriculum which is purely cognitive in content—not by eliminating the cognitive, but by uniting it with the affective. The design begins with a cognitive phase conducted in the classroom, focused on culture, perception, and the concept of culture learning. This is followed by a cross-cultural living experience and a field seminar designed to provide the opportunity for immediate integration of the cognitive and experiential learning. In the final phase, the students return to the classroom to formulate a theoretical framework based on their learning for use in any situation.

LEARNING OBJECTIVES

Based on the assumptions, premises, and theoretical notions given above, which guide the design of cross-cultural study, the overall student learning objectives are twofold: cross-cultural and personal.

The cross-cultural objective is to develop the ability to adapt to and function effectively in cross-cultural situations and thereby become multi-culturally oriented. The personal objective is to become a more flexible, tolerant, and creative person with a different perception of self and others in relation to the world.

The program is designed so that each component makes a specific contribution to achieving these two overall objectives. The processes by which they are attained are by: (a) becoming aware of and correcting one's own cultural as well as personal biases in perception and interpretation of values and behavior; (b) developing sensitivity to cultural differences and recognizing the validity of different values and different ways of meeting life's situations; and (c) developing one's creativity through discovery of alternative solutions to problems.

In sum then, the main objective is not to become a specialist in relation to a given culture but to become a cross-culturally flexible person who can understand and deal comfortably and effectively with people from different cultures. The objectives are refined in the succeeding chapters for each of the three parts of the program.

THE MODEL

The model involves three interdependent curriculum blocks:

I. the pre-field seminar meeting on campus for one two-hour session weekly for a term;

II. the field experience of at least two months in another culture which includes a weekly field seminar and the keeping of a daily journal by the students; and

III. the post-field program on campus which includes two "learning summaries" and weekly meetings during the term following the field experience.

The program extends over 12 to 14 months, depending upon whether the university operates on a quarter or semester system.[22] For academic scheduling it is convenient to have the pre-field seminar in the spring semester or quarter, followed by the field experience in summer. The succeeding fall term accommodates the post-field seminar although the final learning summary is not due until about two months after the seminar ends. The time span requires that, at the latest, undergraduates begin the program in the second half of the junior year—or at community colleges, in the second half of the freshman year. It is suggested that students in professional educational programs begin in the second half of the first year.

GUIDING PRINCIPLES

The basic principles that guide the design are:

- The program is organized so that there is an intermingling of intellectual and experiential learning opportunities.

- The program places students at the center of the educational process, functioning in unstructured situations that require them to evolve their own strategies for making choices, decisions, and evaluations.

- The program, since the goal is multiculturalism, uses a "culture-general" approach to cross-cultural learning (in contrast to "culture-specific" study of a particular other culture). The intent is to help students learn how to discover the structural and functional pattern of any other culture so that they can apply it in a broad range of cross-cultural situations.

---

[22]While the program is described here in the context of college and university instruction, it should be clear that with only minor adaptation it could be implemented in secondary schools as well or for special groups outside the school and academic systems.

• The program design provides students with opportunities to gain insight into the relationship between theory and practice as spiral, not linear.

• The program is designed to avoid closure so that students will maintain the capability for cross-cultural learning throughout their lives.

COMPONENTS

Pre-field Seminar

The rationale for beginning the program with a pre-field seminar emphasizing cognitive learning stems from the belief that some relevant theoretical knowledge of cross-cultural learning will give meaning to observations, reactions, and interactions of students in the field experience—in short, provide a framework for their affective learning. The seminar is planned, also, to help students develop an understanding (at least intellectually) of the nature of both cultural awareness and personal self-awareness. Finally, the seminar is aimed at establishing a mental attitude that will help the students to become active rather than passive learners during the field experience. (The seminar is described in detail in Chapter III.)

Field Experience

The design of the field experience reflects the belief that conscious learning while living in another culture is different from learning about the culture or understanding it cognitively. The field experience provides the hard data which give meaning to the theoretical considerations (the cognitive framework) dealt with in the pre-field seminar.

The students go to an essentially unknown culture with, desirably, the fewest possible preconceptions about how people there behave and what their values and customs are. As the students attempt to find their way in that culture and encounter the problems and ambiguities involved, they experience culture shock.

The process of resolving or recovering from the culture shock is fundamental to the program design, because it helps the students "confront the social-psychological and philosophical discrepancies they find in the new culture as compared to their own cultural props, self-images, and understandings."[23]

---

[23]Adler, 1972, 14.

The guiding principles which underlie the unstructured learning situation in the field are that students (1) have no status or role except that of learner desiring to develop friendships with individuals in the host culture; (2) experience culture shock as an impetus to "unlearn" customary monocultural ways of behaving that do not work in the other culture; (3) seek and discover on their own learning opportunities in which they are required to make choices, decisions, and create alternative ways of problem-solving; in other words, to engage in divergent thinking, and (4) find satisfaction in the pursuit of self-discovery as an end in itself unrelated to the expectations of others. (See Chapter IV for a more detailed discussion of these principles.)

Personal Relationships: It is through developing personal relationships with the people of the host culture that students become culturally self-conscious as they note reactions, however subtle, to their behavior. Uncertainty about the meaning of these reactions, the inability to make immediate interpretations, and the need to find their own learning opportunities create discomfort. A support system is built into the design, namely a daily journal and a weekly field seminar, to prevent students from feeling overwhelmed and depressed and to turn frustration and anxiety into positive learning.

Daily Journal: Students know from the beginning that they will keep a daily journal of their observations, reactions, frustrations, successes, questions, etc. The process of writing the journal requires reflection in order to turn observations and reactions into ideas and conceptual patterns. The journal gives students a means of evaluating their own development and provides content for the field seminar.

Students may wish to pay special attention to some cultural concept that is significant and of interest to them such as the meaning of time, space, possessions/property, nonverbal communication, work-play, and so on, or to a recurrent cultural theme that emerges from their observations. The examination of this theme, however, should not deter them from perceiving the culture as a whole or engaging in a variety of learning pursuits.

Field Seminar: The seminar provides a forum where students can discuss their frustrations and anxieties. It serves also as a channel for gaining a perspective on their experiences and seeing the "connectedness of things." Programming the cognitive process to occur more or less simultaneously with affective learning is educationally potent and proves to be a powerful factor in making this style of learning a habit and in helping the students recognize that learning is (or should be) open-ended and continuous. (See Chapter IV.)

Post-Field Program

The post-field program consists of a seminar and two papers which constitute "learning summaries." This phase of the design is essential because (1) an extended time span, after students are back in their home culture and have taken up daily work and living routines, is needed for conscious reflection on the field learning, so that closure of learning is avoided and new habits of learning become internalized; and (2) time is needed to write the learning summaries which offer students the opportunity to sort out and organize their learning and to evaluate changes in themselves.

Post-field Seminar: This seminar is a time for students to analyze their field learning in retrospect and integrate affective with cognitive learning. New meanings become apparent as this process unfolds.

Summaries: The first summary, written a month after return from the field, may carry on some of the romance of the field learning but for most is primarily a recording of basic learning. The second summary, written about six months later and after the post-field seminar, requires the students to evaluate the learning in perspective, identifying new insights and changes in attitude and discussing how the experience has affected the way they deal with current cross-cultural and other situations.

COGNITIVE LEARNING: THE PRE-FIELD SEMINAR

3

Predeparture orientation seminars are considered by some to be ineffective in preparing students for cross-cultural learning because students report that the orientation has little meaning to them in the field. The problem lies in the fact that most orientation programs deal with the content of the culture rather than the process of learning it. In this design the students are taught how to learn culture and then are put into a situation where they must apply that learning. Even though they tend to be overwhelmed at first by the mass of stimuli confronting them and have difficulty making connections between the ideas from the seminar and their immediate experiences, the students make the connection fairly rapidly under the pressures of their need to learn.

Why not incorporate the theoretical material in the field seminar? There are several reasons. One, learning the theory before going into the field gives time for reflection. Two, the pre-field seminar helps students develop positive attitudes and expectations for the field experience. Three, the students' attention and time in the field should not be spent on cognitive background learning; intellectual effort should be confined to interpreting the field experience within a cognitive framework already in place.

The purposes of the seminar are: (1) to provide a knowledge base, drawn primarily from cultural anthropology and social psychology, that will help students interpret and organize their learning in the field; (2) to help students understand the goals of the program in the context of the design, *i.e.*, why the program is designed in a particular way that is different from the usual study abroad program; and (3) to shake students out of their own comfortable monocultural perceptual systems and start them thinking about themselves in cultural terms.

Students can be expected to come to the seminar with some preconceptions as well as some unformulated, even erroneous, ideas about culture. To some, culture may mean literature, art, and history; to others, a set of customs which can be dealt with by following a list of "do" and "don't" specifics. They may be unprepared to accept the implications or significance of the concept of culture which Melville Herskovits has called "a concept so basic in the human sciences that its discovery and use in the study of man has been compared to the importance of the discovery and use of the concept of gravity in understanding the natural world."[24]

Beyond this, students can be expected to bring varying beliefs about the degree to which behavior is culturally determined, not realizing that it is internalized and has strong emotional as well as cognitive content. As Marshall Singer says,

> The way we perceive the world, what we expect of it, and what we think about it, is so basic and so ingrained, is buried so deep in us and in our unconscious that we continuously act and react without thinking why—without even realizing that we might think why.[25]

Theory in the classroom must be discussed in such a way that students can see its connection, at least dimly, with what they will be doing in the field. Each of the theory sessions should be opened with student discussion and questions about their reading assignments. This approach places considerable responsibility for learning on the students just as it will be in the field. Thus the pre-field seminar can model, at least in some degree, the field seminar.

The use of both in- and out-of-class exercises (see Appendix A) helps students relate theory to their own personal behavior and thus connect the cognitive and affective as they will have to do in the field.

The instructors should have sufficient background in anthropology and social psychology to explain concepts and theories relevant to these topics, as well as sufficient cross-cultural experience to give pertinent examples from real cross-cultural situations.

CULTURE

At the outset instructors should emphasize that the program is designed to produce multiculturally-oriented individuals rather than experts in any

---

[24]Herskovits, 1972, 98.
[25]Singer, 1979, 13–14.

specific culture. Although students go through the experience of learning a particular culture, the built-in ambiguity in the design actually teaches them how to learn any new culture. In other words, the program should prepare students to learn a third or fourth culture with ease and to be able to handle a cross-cultural situation involving any unfamiliar culture. The role of the pre-field seminar in the total program is then explained in relation to the student-learning objectives.

The concept of culture is central to the program and must be introduced early and clearly defined. We like the following definition:

> Culture is the sum total of ways of living, including values, beliefs, esthetic standards, linguistic expression, patterns of thinking, behavioral norms, and styles of communication which a group of people has developed to assure its survival in a particular physical and human environment. Culture and the people who are part of it interact so that culture is not static. Culture is the response of a group of human beings to the valid and particular needs of its members. It, therefore, has an inherent logic and an essential balance between positive and negative dimensions. [26]

While the rules governing our behavior are largely unconscious, we rely on them to interpret and predict others' behavior, just as we rely on the grammatical rules of our native language without being able to verbalize those rules. For instance, most native speakers of English will be at a loss to explain to a foreign student why there has to be the definite article "the" in the expression "go to the hospital" while there is none in "go to school." To be able to give a grammatically convincing explanation, one has to study one's native language and raise the grammatical rules to consciousness. Culture, however, is far more difficult to bring to consciousness than grammar.

> Most of culture lies hidden and is outside voluntary control, making up the warp and weft of human existence. Even when small fragments of culture are elevated to awareness, they are difficult to change, not only because they are so personally experienced but because people cannot act or interact at all in any meaningful way except through the medium of culture. [27]

> The cultural unconscious, those out-of-awareness cultural systems that have as yet to be made explicit, probably outnumber the explicit systems by a factor of one thousand or more. [28]

---

[26]Hoopes, 1979.
[27]Hall, 1966, 188.
[28]Hall, 1976, 166.

Though hidden, these dimensions are shared by other members of the culture thus making life predictable and exerting a stabilizing influence on our lives:

> Culture is the basis of the structure, stability, and security that both individuals and a society must possess if they are to maintain themselves. . . . In essence, culture is the medium through which a society survives and perpetuates itself by the survival, reproduction, and training of the individuals who comprise the society.[29]

The omnipresence and indelibility of culture at a non-conscious level result in people assuming that behavioral norms based on their own culture are universal. Methods and manners of communication are so ingrained in us through our culture that we normally do not even begin to become culturally aware until some kind of cross-cultural communication breakdown occurs and we find that things simply don't mean the same. Even as innocent a greeting as "How are you today?" can be misinterpreted by a foreign visitor who either takes it as very personal or responds with a recital of physical ailments. Samovar, Porter, and Jain make this point crystal clear:

> Culture and communication are inseparable because culture not only dictates who talks with whom, about what, and how the communication proceeds, it also helps to determine how people encode messages, the meanings they have for messages, and the conditions and circumstances under which various messages may or may not be sent, noticed, or interpreted. In fact, our entire repertory of communicative behaviors is dependent largely on the culture in which we have been raised. Culture, consequently, is the foundation of communication. And, when cultures vary, communication practices also vary.[30]

SELECTIVE PERCEPTION

One of the key concepts in the seminar is selective perception, which should be introduced early on so that the students become aware of their cultural and perceptual biases.

A film on visual perception (see Appendix A) that demonstrates how assumptions based on past experience can lead to erroneous interpretations

---

[29]Samovar, Porter, and Jain, 1981, 26.
[30]Samovar, Porter, and Jain, 1981, 26.

in visual illusions is shown to emphasize how strong our perceptual inference habits are.

The symbol perception test developed by Niyekawa (see Appendix A) enables each student to examine the symbols perceived selectively and the reasons for doing so. The students realize that the symbols they tend to recognize—aside from those with structural features, such as size, color, and shape, that made them stand out by contrast—are those with which they are familiar or to which they can give verbal labels. They also recognize individual differences related to varied interests, background, and aesthetic orientations as well as similarities arising from shared backgrounds.

Through slides of figure-ground reversals, it becomes apparent that one cannot focus on both figure and ground at the same time; whatever one focuses on becomes figure and the rest recedes to become background. Thus, by focusing on some aspects of the visual stimuli, we end up screening out the rest. For this reason, perception is always distorted by selectivity (except in the case of an eidetic, *i.e.*, a person with unusually vivid mental images). What one selectively perceives differs according to temporary needs, personality, and culture, apart from the structural aspect inherent in the stimuli. As an example of temporary needs affecting perception, take the students themselves. Because they desire to know more about their country of destination, they tend to notice anything related to it in newspapers, conversations, and so on which previously passed unnoticed.

If temporary needs can have such an influence on selective perception, it is easy to see that enduring needs are likely to have an even greater influence. Projective tests of personality, such as the Thematic Apperception Test or the Rorschach Test, make use of this tendency toward selective perception in individuals. When people of a particular culture share the tendency to perceive certain things selectively, then the selectivity may be considered to be due to cultural influence.

Selective perception is learned without conscious effort. An infant growing up in an English-speaking environment, for instance, learns nonconsciously to ignore the finer difference between the sounds of the letter *p* in *spin* and *pin*, where one *p* is unaspirated and the other is aspirated. Not hearing the difference here does not hinder communication; however, if one does not hear the difference between *p* and *b*, as in *pin* and *bin*, communication is hampered. Thus, we selectively notice whether certain consonants are voiced or not. The strong habits in selective perception of the sounds of one's mother tongue are part of the difficulty in learning to listen to or to speak another language at a later age. These habits constitute interference; they must be unlearned if one is learning a new language.

Cultural difference in the features selectively attended to needs special emphasis. Experiments carried out in different cultures indicate that Westerners are susceptible to certain visual illusions to which people in parts of Africa are not.[31] Geometric figures, these experiments tell us, are perceived differently according to geographic and cultural environment. If that is true, then it can be expected that selectivity and distortion in perception will be greater when the stimulus is something less well structured and more complex or ambiguous, an abstraction, for instance, and when there is room for interpretation, such as in the concept of "honesty" or other aspects of interpersonal behavior. Renato Tagiuri, in his discussion of person perception, points out that:

> . . . in our culture, inferences concerning "honesty," "sincerity," or "gentleness" may be quickly drawn when certain forms of behavior are perceived, while in other cultures, other typologies are used; for example, certain Southwestern Indians wonder first whether the other person does or does not have witchcraft power.[32]

Depending on the value orientation and emphasis within each culture, people in different cultures direct their attention to different aspects of behavior or draw different inferences from the same behavior. For example, a person looking straight into the eyes of the interviewer during an employment interview will be seen as an honest, sincere person in our culture, but as rude and insolent in Japan. We look for different features or patterns of features in judging whether people can be trusted, or in guessing their backgrounds. The features we screen out as irrelevant may turn out to be relevant in another culture. Nonverbal cues are a case in point. Americans, who are direct in their communication, can afford to screen out redundant nonverbal cues, while in cultures where a great deal of communication takes place nonverbally, every minute physical sign becomes relevant. If we have established the habit of ignoring these cues, it takes a conscious effort to take notice of them. Becoming aware of one's selectivity in perception, then, is a first and major step in preparing to learn another culture, for without conscious control of our long established habits, our perception is limited to what is familiar.

Perception involves giving meaning to what one perceives, that is, interpreting it. One sees a four-legged furry animal running away from another four-legged but bigger animal and calls the former a "cat" and the latter a

---

[31]Allport and Pettigrew, 1957; Hudson, 1960; Segall, Campbell, and Herskovits, 1966.
[32]Tagiuri, 1969, 418.

"dog." One sees a little boy pushing another off the see-saw in the park and calls the former an "aggressive" boy. These labels indicate the interpretation given. To call an animal a "dog" or a "cat" or to call a certain behavior aggressive is to categorize them on the basis of specific features. The features that serve as a basis for categorization are the criterial attributes discussed earlier and we tend to focus only on those attributes that are essential for categorizing things and events. Attributes that are non-essential, that is, non-criterial for classification purposes, may escape notice. An example is the aspiration of the letter "p" for speakers of English, as noted above.

Interpretation means to define, understand and make order out of the chaos of the thousands of items in sensory data. It leads to labeling and classifying what is perceived. Each person interprets differently, according to his personality and past experiences, although members of one culture group tend to share basic sets of perceptions which differ from the sets of perceptions shared by members of other culture groups. We establish categories within a system of values and value judgments based largely on the dictates of culture.[33]

Classifying items as "dog" or "tall" or "intelligent" or "aggressive" or "American" or "red" means putting them into discrete categories when actually they may be found on a continuum. This is particularly true when it comes to behavior. Take, for instance, "rude" behavior. When one criticizes another as being rude, a certain kind of behavior, whatever it may be, is labeled "rude." But what constitutes rude behavior? An American businessman meeting a Japanese businessman may, in his eagerness to make a good impression, show extreme friendliness. As soon as he is introduced, he calls the Japanese man by his first name, conducts himself very informally, and occasionally jokes. The Japanese businessman's selective perception, however, is oriented toward evaluating the appropriateness of behavior according to status. Lack of reserve on the part of the American is likely to be interpreted as "rudeness." His smile and his openness may go unnoticed, and on the basis of his relaxed—as opposed to reserved and stiff—behavior, he is classified as impolite.

Once an object or behavior is interpreted, classified, or labeled, the details that make it unique are forgotten and reclassification becomes difficult. If, for that particular culture, this interpretation or classification is erroneous, misunderstandings will follow. Thus for the student going into a new culture, it is important not to interpret or classify too soon. It is better to record in a journal as much detail as possible without labeling or

---

[33]Hoopes, 1979.

classifying, since in the beginning he will be using only criteria from his own culture.

Classifying people into categories and making assumptions about their traits is stereotyping. In other words, stereotyping is classifying a person on the basis of one or two criterial attributes which are assumed to characterize his group—be it race, ethnic group, age, sex, or social class—and then assuming that all attributes associated with that particular category apply to the person. At the same time, the unique characteristics of the individual himself are ignored.

While students are familiar with the concept of stereotyping, they are not likely to admit that they themselves ever engage in it, particularly racial or ethnic stereotyping. This may be true even when they themselves have experienced being stereotyped. Just as the student wants to be seen as an individual rather than as a stereotype, so he must learn to see people of the host culture as individuals and learn to separate individual from cultural traits.

How does one recognize that a trait is unique to an individual and not common to the people of his culture? Obviously, it cannot be done at first meeting. As has been pointed out repeatedly, at this stage the student must keep an open mind and try to perceive as much as possible without automatically screening out what he is accustomed to consider irrelevant or insignificant. Each observation must be kept separate. Labeling and categorizing must be suspended. When certain things are observed repeatedly, when a recurrent pattern is noted, then one may tentatively create a category. As more and more patterns emerge, interrelationships between them may be hypothesized and a cultural framework established. However, until one has had enough exposure to and contact with the people of a new culture, no generalizations should be made.

A discussion of stereotyping will lead to an awareness of the underlying value system and should result in an examination of how such value systems are acquired. Discussion can then move naturally to American culture, cultural bias and cultural delimitation, or monoculturalism.

MONOCULTURALISM

Cultural bias and cultural delimitation are, in a sense, the pivot of the pre-training seminar since they are related to all the previous material as well as to what follows. The purpose is to help the students realize how bound or limited one is by one's own culture and to recognize the advantages of being bi- or multi-cultural.

Through previous discussions of selective perception and categorization, the students should be familiar with the fact that what one perceives from among a multitude of objects and events is selected and that how one interprets and classifies it is influenced by the conventions of the culture in which one grew up.

Speech sounds can be used to show how culture has limited our perceptual abilities. A newborn child is a potential speaker of any language, but he will learn the language spoken around him. An American born in Korea, surrounded by Korean-speaking people, will learn to speak Korean as any Korean would, while a Japanese born in Alabama will learn to speak English with a Southern drawl. The plasticity of the brain which enables the child to learn without conscious effort any language spoken around him is lost by the time he reaches adulthood. Having heard only those speech sounds of his own language and having learned to listen to and make only those differentiations necessary, he will find it difficult to hear crucial differences in speech sounds in another language. We are familiar with the problem that speakers of Japanese have in distinguishing between the letters "l" and "r", with the result that "lice" and "rice" or "glamour" and "grammar" are frequently pronounced in exactly the same way. Similarly, speakers of English have difficulty in hearing the difference between *obasan* and *obaasan* (Japanese kinship terms, one meaning "aunt," the other, "grandmother," but frequently used as terms of address) and consequently pronounce the two words in the same way. Usually, the one with a short vowel is used to address an adult woman (up to middle age) and the one with the long vowel to address an old woman, but, because vowel length is not a criterial attribute in English, speakers of English have difficulty in perceiving the difference in sounds. Students have little difficulty understanding this point, having had sufficient experience learning a foreign language in high school and hearing foreign accents.

This is the point at which Guilford's idea of convergent *vs.* divergent thinking should be introduced, along with Maslow's concept of the two forces which drive human beings—safety and growth.

According to Maslow:

> Every human being has both sets of forces within him. One set clings to safety and defensiveness out of fear, tending to regress . . . hanging on to the past. . . . The other set of forces impels him forward toward wholeness of Self and uniqueness of Self, toward full functioning of all his capacities, toward confidence in the face of the external world at the same time accepting his deepest, real unconscious Self. . . .

> Therefore we can consider the process of healthy growth to be a neverending series of free choice situations, confronting each individual at every point throughout his life, in which he must choose between the

delights of safety and growth, dependence and independence, regression and progression, immaturity and maturity. Safety has both anxieties and delights; growth has both anxieties and delights. We grow forward when the delights of growth and anxieties of safety are greater than the anxieties of growth and the delights of safety.[34]

Maslow's "never-ending series of free choice situations" can be brought closer to home by giving examples from our daily lives. For instance, we tend to choose the quickest and surest way of doing things because we do not want to waste time or money. We tend to take the same route every day to work or school rather than to explore different routes occasionally which might be refreshing or might lead us into a traffic jam. When we give a child his first camera we tell him not to take just any picture but to be selective because we do not want to waste expensive color films. Oriented to be efficient and practical, we do not allow ourselves to try new ways of accomplishing things. Repetition makes these ways habitual. In other words, the force for safety tends to win out over the force for growth.

In Guilford's two concepts of cognitive modes, the force for safety can be related to convergent thinking, which, as noted above tends toward retaining the known, learning the predetermined and conserving what is, while the force for growth is related to divergent thinking, which tends toward revising the known, exploring the undetermined, and constructing what might be.[35] The formal educational system as well as the home and social environment tend to encourage convergent thinking, as was discussed in the previous chapter. We get constant reinforcement for making the "right" judgment or "correct" prediction based on limited cues, for making logical deductions based on facts, and for behaving appropriately according to cultural expectations. In general, we do not receive the same kind of reinforcement if we deviate from others, if we use imagination rather than rational thinking or take the risk of trying something new. It is important at this point to help the students examine how people are confined by their own cultures and value systems. For instance, in American culture, privacy, personal freedom, independence, equality and other important values assumed to be universal by mainstream Americans, may be found to rank lower than harmony, cooperation, and self-control in other cultures, including those of some minority groups in the U.S.[36]

---

[34]Maslow, 1956, 37–38.

[35]Guilford, 1959.

[36]Different approaches are possible in discussing this subject. Miner's *Nacirema* (1956) may serve as a good eye opener. Stewart's *American Cultural Patterns: A Cross-cultural Perspective* (1971) is useful in analyzing American cultural assumptions and values and comparing cultural pat-

Within these confines we tend to find safety, security, and reward by following the established way. Not only do we become used to doing things in the culturally acceptable way, we also come to think that these are the only ways or, more obviously judgmental, the right ways. In fact, it would never occur to some people that alternative ways are possible. This is cultural bias, which has a blinding effect that we call cultural delimitation.

We are taught from early childhood that stealing is bad, and we teach our children the same. A teacher who has a Samoan child in her class constantly receives complaints from the other children that this child has stolen a pencil or ball or book. The teacher tells the Samoan child that it is bad to steal and that he must stop taking other people's possessions. The child is confused and says that he is simply sharing. The teacher discusses the problem with someone who knows the Samoan culture and learns that in the Samoan culture everything is shared among relatives and friends and that personal ownership is not known. The teacher explains this to the other children but it has no effect. They still maintain that taking things that belong to someone else is stealing and is bad. What they have not discovered is that if they borrow something from the Samoan child he will not expect it to be returned. Thus the positive aspect of the Samoan custom is overlooked. The American, resentful at having something "stolen" from him, is reacting emotionally and cannot accept the fact that this is normal behavior in Samoa. Reclassifying the Samoan child's behavior from "stealing" to "sharing" is not possible, and the behavior, as well as the child, is rejected.

CROSS-CULTURAL LEARNING

While the previous topic focused on how biased the perspective of a monocultural person is and how culture binds the person and limits his potentials, cross-cultural learning shows the way to overcoming the limitations imposed by culture.

At the heart of cross-cultural learning is the process of coming to grips with differences and learning to cope with ambiguity, the ultimate goal being the ability to function comfortably and effectively in a new culture. The first step toward achieving that goal is cultural awareness, not merely at the intellectual level of understanding, but at the affective level as well.

---

terns of thinking and behaving. *The Ugly American* (Lederer and Burdick, 1958) reveals how American culture may be perceived by people outside the United States.

The difficulty in becoming aware of the things that one takes for granted was pointed out earlier. We need oxygen to survive, but, because it is all around us, we do not notice it until we are deprived of it. The best way to become aware of how culture-bound we are is to step out of our own culture. If we follow our customary ways in another culture, we soon find out that misunderstanding and miscommunication result. By being hurt or embarrassed as a result of these misunderstandings—by going through culture shock—we are made aware of our own cultural ways and how ingrained they are. As time passes and we develop deeper personal relationships with people in the host culture, we begin to recognize not only that there are different ways of doing the same thing, but that for the most part there is as much "rightness" in their way, within their cultural context, as there is in ours. We also learn to look at things from the other culture's point of view. In other words, we come to grasp the nature of cultural relativity.

In the process we will probably have gone through a minor identity crisis, since our self-image and identity are closely tied to many of the cultural traits on which we have had to loosen our grip. We will have been forced to re-examine who we are and re-affirm ourselves in a much more fundamental way than is possible when we are immersed in and reinforced by our own culture. We will also have experienced the personal growth involved in learning new ways. We will be better equipped to become what Maslow calls the "self-actualizing person."

At this point in the seminar it is useful to introduce the idea of the authoritarian personality and contrast it with that of the self-actualizing person. The authoritarian personality tends to act on the basis of external authority and to think in a linear, convergent fashion. The self-actualizing person is creative, characterized by the inclination to engage in divergent thinking and the ability to break out of the conventions imposed by society and formal education.

On home ground, as we repeat the things we are sure will work smoothly or that we enjoy, we limit our range of activities and interests and become set in our ways. When the students go into a new culture where their only objective is to learn the culture, they will have to explore and find out the surest and best way to get things done according to new standards. In the process they may discover new joys and pleasures as well as disappointments. In other words, the force for safety that makes one cling to the past has little chance of winning out over the force for growth. The students will be forced to correct their biased perceptions, at least sufficiently to recognize the significant and relevant aspects of the new culture. They will have to engage in divergent thinking because the conventional way of interpreting behaviors and events will not work. They will be forced to exercise the type of behavior associated with the non-authoritarian, creative personality.

The discussion of cross-cultural learning in these sessions is, from one perspective, an integrating process because it creates a sense of wholeness; at the same time, it is anxiety-producing because it focuses on what students themselves will be doing in the field. Although they are now eagerly anticipating the experience, they are aware that they have no "map" of exactly what to do.

FIELD ORIENTATION

As the end of the semester approaches, students are eager to concentrate on practical concerns as they prepare for the field. Therefore, the last two sessions are devoted to field methodology and field orientation.

The purpose of the discussion about field methodology is essentially to guide the students as to what to include in their journals. The students are encouraged to record all kinds of observations in their journals. It should be pointed out to them that in the beginning one tends to notice things that are the most different and stand in sharp contrast to one's own culture, without seeing that within the broad categories there are finer differentiations.

In a certain culture, for instance, gratitude may be expressed in such a way that the newcomer notices it. Later he may learn that what he thought was one type of behavior was actually two, which were outwardly much alike. Until he became aware of certain nuances, however, he had no way of knowing that one was an expression of gratitude and the other an apology. Obviously, the students' journals will change over a period of time as they learn the cues and perceive the nuances.

Preparing students to be perceptive observers is important. This calls for breaking through the screening (selective perceptual) habits derived from one's own culture in order to avoid classifying behavior in inappropriate categories. They are encouraged in the beginning to record observations and experiences in their journals without interpretation, classification, or evaluation. Things that seemed unimportant at the time they were recorded later take on unexpected significance—and vice versa.

They should be instructed in active listening skills. In pursuing cross-cultural learning one does not just listen, one listens for something. Listening to silence or for non-verbal cues or variations in voice intonation can be as informative as listening to words and sentences. People say a great deal about themselves and their feelings and attitudes through these forms of communication.

37

It is also important to learn how to ask questions in a way that stimulates conversation rather than eliciting conversation-stopping pieces of information. Direct questions may, in addition, result in answers which tell you what the person thinks he is supposed to think or what he believes you want to hear. Small talk, indirect questions and questions that arise out of listening carefully to the other person are more effective modes.

This approach to seeking, recording, and later analyzing experience involves divergent thinking and may contrast dramatically with some other cross-cultural research that tends toward convergent styles. Often in cross-cultural studies hypotheses are developed by Westerners and measures for the data are set in terms of Western culture. Frequently, however, the measures chosen, though important in Western culture, are not so important in the other culture. The findings, therefore, do not reflect very much of the new culture.

When one assumes universality or assumes that people should place a certain value on some particular behavior or habit, such as openness or frankness, it often happens that one ends up measuring something that is not even there. When one is looking for something, it is generally found, but whether or not what is found is an important ingredient of the other culture is open to question.

The last session of the seminar is devoted to providing essential information on the field site and answers to questions regarding the trip. Information about the culture-communication styles, behavior patterns, values, and assumptions is kept to a minimum so that students enter the new culture with as few preconceptions as possible. Factual information is provided on the historical background of the people, language, religion, form of government, geography, climate, clothing, types of transportation available, main economic base, and the like. In addition students are given information about housing arrangements, health insurance, procedures for being introduced to community representatives, and other details, as well as about any cultural rules that must be observed if they are not to be ostracized from the moment they arrive.

Many of the students' questions will reveal their anxieties. Some, such as how to behave in a particular situation, should not be answered. The students should be told, "This you will find out yourself. That is part of the learning." Other queries such as how much and what type of clothing to take, can be given straight answers.

The general learning objectives of the pre-training seminar are not fully achieved and recognized by the students until later. By the end of the seminar the students hopefully have some knowledge, some theory, an attitude of sensitivity, and an intellectual readiness for uncertainty, although they are likely to be anxious about their ability to handle the uncertainty. Intellectually, they know that the instructors are trying to help them avoid preconceptions and a rigid "mental set" before going into the new culture, which has helped them develop an intellectual tolerance for unstructured responses to their specific questions about the host culture, but the lack of structure is nevertheless difficult for them.

The final question-and-answer period heightens their excitement and prepares them for departure, which should take place within two to three weeks of the final session to take advantage of the momentum of their anxiety and anticipation.

4 EXPERIENTIAL LEARNING: THE FIELD EXPERIENCE

We regard experiential learning as the core element in culture learning. Both cognitive and affective learning are involved; actually a unity of the two is sought in the "internalization process [which] represents a continuous modification of behavior from the individual's being aware of a phenomenon to a pervasive outlook on life that influences all his actions."[37] That is the usual process, but learning a second culture appears to be qualitatively different. It appears to involve not only learning to make finer differentiations in formerly undifferentiated wholes (*i.e.*, to make continuous modifications) but also being sufficiently shaken up to recognize that certain previously learned role behavior differentiations are not useful and must be ignored or forgotten in order to learn new ones.

An illustration of this kind of learning need may be seen in parents who want to help their children with their homework but cannot because they are not familiar with the new ways of teaching reading, or spelling, or the "new math." The ways they learned as children are dysfunctional in this situation. Similarly, in learning a new culture one is forced to ignore and forget old dysfunctional patterns of differentiations and to engage in learning new ones. This ego-involving experience requires considerable risk to one's self-esteem.

In 1967, Harrison and Hopkins, writing about goals of cross-cultural learning, said the learner must not only "solve new problems in a new setting, but he must develop a new learning style, quite on his own. This

---

[37]Krathwohl, *et. al.*, 1956, 33.

41

experience—not knowing how to learn without traditional supports—may be productive of a good deal of anxiety and depression grouped under the rubric culture shock." They go on to say that "if the trainee can be educated to be an effective and independent learner he need not be filled with all the information he can contain before going into his new job. . . . He will have the capacity to generate his own learning as needed."[38]

Harrison and Hopkins suggest that another dimension in cross-cultural learning is "the extent to which the emotions, values, and deeper aspects of the self are actively involved, touched, and changed in the learning process." They point out that it is not possible to maintain "emotional distance from the sights, the smells, the sounds, and the customs of an alien culture." The supportive aspects of one's own culture are absent, which is emotionally disruptive, and "one's assumptions and values are called into question again and again by the most trivial kinds of events. The interpersonal competencies that work well in one's own culture suddenly do not work any more. The cues are different. One can avoid the encounter only by retreating into some kind of physical or emotional enclave, into the kinds of American compounds that wall off Yankees from natives all over the world."[39]

An important objective in this cross-cultural learning is the development of the ability and willingness to take some emotional risks in situations where one's sense of self-esteem is involved. Harrison and Hopkins proposed alternative approaches to risk-taking:

> Low-risk alternatives might include withdrawal from the relationship or resort to written rather than oral communication. High-risk alternatives might include retaliation with some kind of personal attack. . . . The low- and high-risk approaches allow the cause of the situation to remain unknown and not dealt with. They are designed more to ease the tension and uncertainty than to solve the problem.[40]

The moderate-risk approach, however, involves willingness to increase tension in order to obtain information about the situation. Moderate-risk approaches "require more ability to stand emotional tension over a period of time than do the others."

The moderate-risk approach is recommended for this program. The ability to learn independently and the willingness to take emotional risks appear to be interdependent components in the development of one's own creativity, as the term is used here. This type of cross-cultural learning is

---

[38]Harrison and Hopkins, 1967, 439.
[39]Ibid., 440.
[40]Ibid., 441.

transferable to other circumstances. The participants can therefore be expected to deal with the ambiguities and uncertainties of living and working in any situation.

ASSUMPTIONS

The field learning experience is designed with the idea of developing a new style of learning. The broad goals for a student are to learn to communicate with people of another culture on their own ground (which implies learning the culture) and, in the process, to develop an awareness of his own cultural frame of reference and behavior, to develop his own creativity in communication, ways of seeing situations, solving problems, and so on. The learner can then move toward biculturality, that is, toward the kind of learning that can be transferred for use in various other cultural or subcultural situations.

Some of the assumptions underlying the project design are:

1. Culture shock is an essential ingredient of culture learning; while it can be damaging to the individual if he is so unprepared as to find the shock traumatic, it can, in smaller doses, be an effective instrument of learning in that it appears to shake the individual out of his fixed cultural frame of mind. Peter Adler, in fact, argues that "culture shock and the notion of a cross-cultural learning experience are essentially the same phenomenon, the difference being the scope of focus or view."[41]

2. It is the emotional ego-involving experience of success and failure as well as the temporary loss of role identity that makes the learning from living in another culture different from learning about the culture from lectures, books, films, and simulated exercises.

3. At home, other people's expectations of us make the process of "breaking the habit" more difficult. Family and friends reinforce habits, customary ways of behaving, values, and even our own expectations of ourselves. For this reason a field site distant from home facilitates learning and change.

4. An equal status relationship with people of the other culture is an important ingredient in the kind of learning that is projected.

5. A culture-general approach as opposed to a culture-specific approach is more effective in developing transferable learning skills.

6. Developing a new style of learning and creativity in problem-solving requires opportunities to experiment and to risk oneself in unstructured, uncertain situations that demand problem-solving efforts in the face of

---

[41]Adler, 1972, 6–7.

inadequate knowledge or conflicting information (ambiguity).

7. Some supports, both psychological and environmental, are needed in order for positive learning to occur in an unstructured environment, ambiguous situation, and/or an unknown setting.

Obviously, students will learn in a variety of ways but the three types of learning activities considered essential involve students in (1) discovering opportunities on their own and making contacts with people in the host culture, including initiating, developing, and sustaining friendships with a few people; (2) keeping a daily journal; and (3) participating in a weekly field seminar.

THE FIELD LEARNING PROCESS

Stages of Learning

For each individual the field experience is filled with the unexpected, with unpremeditated insights, intuitive leaps, and experimentation.

Nevertheless, based on our experience with students from both American (a cosmopolitan mix of ethnic groups in Hawaii) and Hong Kong Chinese cultures, the learning can be expected to move through four fairly definable stages.

The first stage, of just over two weeks for most students, is characterized by what might be called disorganization; the second stage, approximately a week, is one of re-examination and reflection; the third stage (fourth and fifth weeks, spilling over into the sixth) seems to be one of reorganization; and the last stage (sixth through eighth week) is characterized by the emergence of new perspectives.[42]

The first stage is characterized by disorientation, anxiety, acute feelings of physical and personal discomfort, difficulty in making decisions, and frustration because usual ways of behaving do not work.

Expressions of frustration include annoyance, even irritation and exasperation, as well as confusion and puzzlement. There are, of course, positive reactions, especially to people they meet or to specific experiences.

Decisions, large or small, tend to be difficult for the students, and the reactions of most of them to cultural situations involving differing values tend to be strong and are usually expressed negatively. Many will probably experience anxiety and a temporary loss of self-esteem. Not having an

---

[42]See Appendix B for a detailed analysis of these stages based on the verbal and written reactions of the students.

instrumental role may be a significant factor in the sense of inadequacy. Again, there will be distinct variations in the expression of this sense of loss.

Toward the end of this stage "unlearning" begins. Dabrowski refers to this process as "positive disintegration," a phenomenon which occurs when the individual is in disharmony with both himself and his environment. Dabrowski believes that "no growth takes place without previous disintegration."[43]

The second stage (the third week) is one of re-examination and reflection, of "taking stock." There appears to be a gentle shift in the learning process along with strong feelings of ambivalence. Students need to stay at home or to be alone for periods of time. They engage in more reflection and less "doing" than in the previous weeks. Some colds, upset stomachs, or other physical problems continue, but there is less frustration and it is felt with less intensity. Observations and comments about the culture tend to be neutral, sprinkled with some positive and some negative comparisons with their own culture. Students portray a sense of readiness to explore what is not understood and some awareness of their own cultural biases.

Most will find a friend or family with whom they feel at ease and to whom they can talk. For those who don't make this kind of contact, frustration may remain high.

Given some variation, most students will show an increased awareness of their own cultural values. Handling the initial period of culture shock—of ambiguity, uncertainty, and temporary loss of identity—and learning that they can risk enough to develop relationships with people of another culture may be significant factors in this shift in attitude.

The third stage is one of reorganization marked by the emergence of new feelings about both their own and the host culture. There is a gain in confidence which enables them to take greater risks. They become more thoroughly and genuinely involved in relationships with people in the host culture. Earlier confusions about "active and passive understanding" and the nature of affective learning begin to clear up, and students feel fully involved in learning. Cultural observations reflect an acceptance of differences and an eagerness to get more deeply into the host culture. Students tend to feel they are not "outsiders" although they are not yet "insiders" either.

In the fourth stage (sixth through eighth week) a coalesence of experience occurs and new perspectives emerge. Students are both putting together the pieces of their experience and evaluating it. Here are some of the changes and developments that can be detected during this period: (1)

---

[43]Dabrowski, 1964, xiv.

frustrations are those which accompany a desire to increase learning; (2) students tend to be acutely aware of changes in their attitudes and outlooks; (3) they experience marked satisfaction in their host culture relationships; (4) most will have sufficient understanding of the culture to recognize how little they know but also how much they have learned; (5) they will be, at least intellectually, prepared to generalize from this knowledge and experience to other cultures and subcultures; (6) they will have an expanded awareness of their own cultures and be ready to engage in reexamining and evaluating aspects that they had previously taken for granted and/or considered universal; and (7) they will be able to articulate some of these new perspectives.

Not all will be satisfied with their learning, but they will have much more confidence in their abilities and be prepared to take greater risks in their interactions. They also recognize the significance of the learning process in which they have been involved and the new style of learning they are beginning to use. They know that an active understanding of a culture is essential to cross-cultural communication.

In reviewing their experience they can see changes in themselves by contrasting how they felt at the beginning of the project with how they see themselves at the end. Some will be disappointed in not having met their expectations and will work especially hard to do so during this period.

Cultural Adjustment Cycle

Participants of a program which allocates eight weeks to the field (overseas) experience, as this design recommends, will probably find, as we did, that the cultural adjustment cycle did not follow the typical patterns identified by Sverre Lysgaard in his pioneering study of Norwegian student in the U.S.[44] His U-curve adjustment cycle starts off with a honeymoon period of seemingly easy adjustment and moves "down" the curve to anxiety and disorganization before turning up again as a more substantive adjustment occurs. The students in the experimental project did not seem to experience any honeymoon, moving instead almost directly into a state of disorientation and stress. It may be that the pre-field seminar enabled them to give full vent to the excitement which, for many, is the principal feeling during the first days or weeks of an overseas experience. It may also be that the seminar so effectively prepared the students for culture shock that the element of innocence required to make the honeymoon work was not present.

---

[44]Lysgaard, 1955. There have been a number of adaptations and revisions of Lysgaard's analysis, but we feel his original formulation holds up well.

A program in which the field experience is longer may encounter a curious phenomenon that has been noted by a number of students of culture shock: the phases of culture shock tend to stretch out to accommodate the length of the stay. The person who spends a year overseas will not find his culture shock and adjustment tribulations compressed into six weeks and enjoy ten and a half months of bicultural tranquility. The culture shock/adjustment phase will instead stretch out to three or four months or more.

The Field Seminar

At the start of the field seminar students may tend to assume the customary role of learner. They may seek assurances that they are doing "satisfactory work" in their journals, the field, and so on. It is not comfortable to relinquish this need for being evaluated in these terms or break their dependence on an educational structure no matter how it confines learning. Culture shock frustrations are high, and a structure that uses current experiential learning as its content adds yet another temporary frustration. The cumulative feelings of frustration and confusion are usually expressed negatively; the students may accuse the faculty member of what they consider to be poor planning, and/or blame the host culture. If there is trust among students and between the students and faculty member, students feel free to challenge the faculty member and each other.

But if the field seminar is to be an effective framework within which to draw learning from experience, then it needs a looseness of structure in which paramount attention may be given to the unique experiences of the individual participants. The discussions in the seminar provide the opportunity for the students to think and emote through their experiences and obtain different perspectives from other students and faculty. Occasional frustrations, eruptions of feeling and challenges to understanding provide fertile ground for learning.[45] The experiences and feelings lead directly into attempts to unravel the mysteries of the host culture and/or to comprehend how they as representatives of their own culture are affecting their hosts.

The daily journal kept by the students plays an important part both in the field experience as a whole and specifically in the field seminar. At any given moment, the journal functions as a psychological support enabling the students to release negative feelings and articulate positive learning; it

---

[45]Note that the focus is on the experience in and with the host culture, not on the experience in the seminar. This seminar is not an encounter group and should not be allowed to become one.

catches the essence of the experience "on the wing," so to speak, which is difficult to do later; and it forces them to reflect immediately, and in some degree systematically, on their experiences. It may produce insights at the moment or later upon rereading, and it usually provides an objective record of personal growth. When asked, "How did you see this earlier?" one student said, "I can't answer that fully until I review my journal."

The journal also serves as an educational tool for the field seminar. Students read each other's journals before each seminar session.[46] This exchange of journals can have great impact as students discover themselves interpreting and reacting to the same experience in quite different ways and from different personal and cultural perspectives. It serves as a strong stimulus to discussion in the seminar as students challenge each other. The exchange of journals does not appear to inhibit them in being frank and open in their descriptions and assessments of their experiences.

It is the function of the instructor to help the students translate their feelings and insights into conceptualizations which throw light on (1) their own culture and culture-based behaviors, (2) the culture and behaviors of their hosts, and (3) the nature of the interaction between them. Ultimately the students should be able to at least begin to analyze their experiences in terms of such cross-cultural issues as depersonalization, differing concepts of time, the doing/being dichotomy, friendship patterns, individualism, directness, etc.

---

[46]If the group is as large as 10 students, they might read half the journals one week and the other half the next week to get a mix.

INTEGRATION: THE POST-FIELD PROGRAM

5

The post-field program spans approximately seven to eight months and has two parts: the post-field seminar and two written "summaries of learning" from each student. The first summary is written one month following return from the field experience and prior to the beginning of the seminar; the second and final summary is written about six months later.

During this phase of the program the students are given the opportunity to review the total learning experience and, especially, to connect the pre-field seminar to the field experience.

They can now understand more fully the function of the pre-field seminar: to give them, as one student put it, a new "mental set," a way of viewing and dealing with cross-cultural experience.

But that mental set does not automatically come into play in the field. Early in the field learning the students are painfully aware of not knowing what to do or how to behave. At the same time, they are so fatigued by the many stimuli and by coping with the changes in their immediate day-to-day living that they tend to forget the pre-training. They are unable to connect the problems related to their daily living with culture learning. Part way through the field learning, with an occasional reminder from the field instructor, they begin to remember and use the pre-training concepts (*e.g.*, non-verbal communication, etc.) which help them to organize isolated incidents and observations into possible patterns so they can arrive at new questions and ideas.

Thus, the value of the pre-training (primarily a cognitive approach) becomes apparent in the field and, later, in the "integration" seminar when the major concepts are reviewed.

Students are able to reflect on how much of a "total experience" the field training was. As one of the students pointed out, "In the field one can't go home at five o'clock, close the book, and walk away from people. You are constantly reminded that you are in another culture and that it is always with you. It is this awareness—you can't turn it off. You can't shut off the things that are uncomfortable and think about them later. They are part of you every minute." And another: "We were forced to make use tomorrow of what we had learned today, so things 'stuck'. Back home one can retreat."

The field seminar, too, is brought into perspective during the integration process. The students can now understand clearly that its function was to help them get beyond discomfort and to organize and interpret their experiences. It created a milieu for divergent thinking where they could explore differences in observations and interpretations of the same incident or experience.

The post-field program enables the students to re-interpret, integrate, and formulate their learning into a whole experience. It enables them to stand back and see the structure or connectedness of things. It also helps them avoid closure at a time when they are still uncertain about the new concepts and consciousness they have been exploring within themselves. It is important for the students to keep the learning alive and moving; they cannot, as happens too frequently with a course, finish and say, "Well, that was an interesting experience." Learning has just begun and should not be filed away and regarded as complete.

The student summaries serve important objectives. The first summary, written soon after they return, enables the students to assess the experience from a distance and especially to explore the more obvious changes which have taken place inside them. In the second summary, written six months later, issues dealt with in the post-field seminar are further reinforced, helping students achieve a greater depth of analysis. They are able to discuss how the experience has affected them and been integrated into their daily lives.

The post-field or integration seminar is, in effect, a continuation of the field seminar and is essentially a reinforcing experience. It offers an opportunity to re-examine and reinterpret learning experiences.

The early sessions may be devoted to a review of concepts presented during the pre-training period. Then follows a re-examination and re-interpretation of the students' cultural learning and personal growth and some practice in divergent thinking.

It is important to provide the students at this point with a theoretical framework for understanding culture which was not previously introduced.

We use the schema developed by Edward Hall in *The Silent Language* which includes the idea of primary message systems and the concept that man operates continuously on three different levels of culture: the formal, the informal, and the technical, shifting frequently among the three.[47]

A different framework of analysis could be used, but we found that Hall's comprehensive scheme, especially the ten message systems, meshes well with the areas of student learning.

They need a bit of help at the beginning in understanding that each message system can accommodate a variety of behavioral situations which reflect the prevalent values of a culture but are not mentioned specifically in Hall's description. These ten basic areas of human activity are elaborated sufficiently by Hall, however, to give students a solid handle on the idea.

By developing a living model of the field culture, using the analytical framework above, students become aware of how theory and practice are intertwined; they see the order, consistency (as well as inconsistency) and cohesiveness of the culture—they see the "whole" in perspective. They also find useful a comparison of their perceptions of the culture with existing studies.

The seminar now shifts focus slightly to an examination of the supernatural. Beliefs, stories, and legends are value carriers in all cultures; studying them can help students better identify, in their real-life experiences, manifestations of some of the basic values of a society.

During the field experience students begin to recognize that supernatural beliefs—in the form of legends, myths, folk tales, etc.—are related to values but there is little time to explore them beyond asking a few questions and making a few superficial observations. The role of supernatural beliefs comes into focus in the study of the framework of culture, and students realize that legends are powerful sources of values. Devoting a relatively brief period of time for focused discussion helps students move toward an active understanding that legends are a major carrier of tradition and that the values they project, albeit symbolically, both reflect and help to shape everyday life. Consciously, most students seem to know little about supernatural beliefs and about the legends that portray them and

---

[47]See page 74 for a further discussion of the use of Hall's model.

have given little thought to those on which some of our own values may be based.[48]

Following the exploration of one or more legends from the target culture, a brief comparative study of legends from several cultures gives a useful perspective.

The sessions in the latter part of the seminar should be a summing up of the total experience, including (a) re-examination of the methods of learning used in the field experience—observations, listening, asking questions, problem-solving, developing personal relationships, reflection, recording, and analyzing experience; (b) comparison of earlier and current perceptions of members of the culture; (c) examination of the students' view of the world; and (d) examination of the extent to which all of the above permeates their work and daily living. This discussion tends to reinforce partially formed habits.

We want here to summarize briefly the overall outcomes of a program in cross-cultural learning. They lie principally in five areas: cultural awareness, culture learning skills, interpersonal skills, communication skills and personal growth.

Cultural Awareness. The students come to understand the meaning of cultural relativity and grasp the concept of culture. They become aware of the degree to which their behaviors are determined by culture. They recognize that cultures have an internal consistency and can be appreciated for their differences. Cultural awareness sensitizes them to cross-cultural elements in their own immediate environment as well as freeing them to function comfortably and effectively in cross-cultural situations involving unfamiliar cultures.

Culture Learning Skills. Culture learning, of course, is the principal subject of this book and has been discussed extensively. For most people, spending time living in another culture would result in some degree of culture learning. What this design offers is a way to systematize that learning, translate it into skills that can be transferred to other cross-cultural situations, and, in the process, further the development in the individual of multicultural or, at least, cross-cultural competencies.

Interpersonal Skills. The program stresses the pursuit of cross-cultural learning through interpersonal relations. As the students explore the foreign cultural environment and different ways of perceiving and behaving, they learn new and more effective ways to connect with other human beings.

Communication Skills. And, of course, they have to learn intercultural communication skills in the process. They learn that communication and

---

[48]See Appendix A for more detail on this aspect of the seminar.

culture are closely intertwined and that "learning the culture" is as important as knowing the language spoken.

Personal Growth. Finally, the students gain confidence in themselves and a strengthened sense of identity and self-esteem. This includes a new tolerance for ambiguity, a flexibility in daily living and a willingness to seek alternative meanings in their interactions with people.

ANALYSIS OF LEARNING: 6 THE GUAM EXPERIENCE

We feel that the best way to examine the nature of the learning that occurs in this design is to discuss it in the context of a specific experience. The Guam program is eminently suited to that purpose.

Each student perceived some changes in himself as a result of his participation in the project—all in the direction of growth. The changes varied in quality, degree, and area of learning.

All of the students appeared to have blended cognitive and affective learning well enough to use it in subsequent situations in their regular social work practicum, as well as to exhibit certain changes in behavior. Negative responses to systems in the new culture that were quite different from their own gradually evolved into an attitude of appreciation and respect. This change was apparent in increased awareness of non-verbal communication; increased ability in subsequent communication with people in other cultures or subcultures as well as in their own; greater flexibility and increased tolerance for ambiguity shown in a more relaxed and confident approach to situations in daily living and to seemingly difficult problems; and an understanding of cultural relativity. At the end of the eight weeks in Guam, however, they did not believe that they had yet acquired a good understanding of the basic philosophy of the new culture or that they could comprehend the meaning of the pattern as a whole.

The learning experience of the students substantiates the notion that one's culture shapes and structures one's life and behavior in subtle and consistent ways. The concept of time is a good illustration as it was by far the most pervasively frustrating aspect of the students' learning.

55

Americans tend to do one thing at a time (when they work, it is work; when they play, it is play) and this requires scheduling. Time is understood in segments (50 minutes, an hour, and so on); it is seen as linear and goals are set in relation to explicitly stated amounts of time (the job should be finished by four o'clock; it is time for the next person's appointment). Appointments are important. Time is an essential controlling and ordering factor in industrialized countries, and activities are compartmentalized. This dominates not only business but our social relations as well. In this sense, it sets priorities in our lives since we select in relation to time what we will perceive.

The students became aware of the importance of time in their culture when, according to the standards of their culture, they initially had no "schedule" in Guam. They found it difficult to make decisions about their activities, such as what they would do when and where or when, where, and what they would eat. They reacted as though their way of seeing and using time was the right way.

Their miscommunications and frustrations led them to learn that Guamanians operated with a different perception of time which was part of a larger cultural context. In this process they learned a great deal about their own system and gained perspective on it.

They found that Guamanians normally do not do one thing at a time. They work and play at the same time. Appointments are not important, nor are schedules, except in certain bureaucratic organizations where people have learned the American concept of time. The work and play phenomenon appeared to the students to emphasize involvement of people as people rather than as workers. They realized that a task was to be completed but not within a scheduled time. No matter how long the line of customers, the clerk is involved with the person she is helping, and completing a transaction satisfactorily with that person is important. Efficiency does not have priority as a value; interpersonal relationships do.

The students had achieved a new outlook on a pervasive dominant system of their own culture. They could evaluate and recognize some patterns in their own culture about which they now raised questions without passing judgment on either culture. Most did speak of things they wanted to modify personally, however, where they thought time had become their master.

Students recognized the broad implications of these two fundamentally different systems of time in professional practice as well as in their peronal lives. One student reflected:

> . . . what I called "inefficiency" at the beginning . . . was my category for what I could see later as a . . . more relaxed pace of life. [Perhaps] this

did not show itself so much while in Guam because I remained somewhat more uptight about "getting things done" than some of the others. But since I am back at home, I have been able to test myself against my previous "reality." I feel more relaxed and am not so anxious about having things just right. . . . I see how future-oriented we are. We rarely allow ourselves to live for today, nor can we be content with "being" rather than "doing." We . . . plan everything from what to do next year on vacation to what to do after dinner tonight to what we want children to be 20 years from now. . . . It occurs to me now that I have rarely passed a day in my life when I did not "accomplish" something until now. I also rarely gave myself the opportunity to reflect on much of what was happening in my life. I wonder whether many Americans do. . . . We really are slaves of the clock.

One might anticipate that the students would give considerable attention to patterns of interpersonal relationships since they were expected to develop non-instrumental relationships with Guamanians as part of learning the culture. In this context, culture learning and personal development were interdependent.

At first, the students categorized the Guamanian family as an "extended family system" and took for granted that they knew what this meant. For some time they made segmental observations, such as Guamanians pay great respect to older people; the husband-wife relationship is different from that in our culture; the older children take responsibility at an early age for young children; children get a great deal of attention from all members of the family; children enjoy going to visit their grandparents on Sunday; many grown, married children go to see their parents every day or so; people who meet for the first time begin by identifying themselves according to family and then conversation flows; youth are supposed to do what their parents want them to, *e.g.*, with respect to dating. They observed that children and youth, and perhaps adults as well, were reluctant to draw attention to themselves as individuals ("I'm shame to go on the dance floor until others are dancing"). Actually this was so for some of our students as well. Students quickly became aware of the warmth and caring in relationships among the Guamanians and of the quality of sharing. They recognized that family, church, and community or village are integrated and are determinants in the system of stable, close relationships.

All of these observations initially were just that: bits and pieces of information. After a while the students began to see that Guamanians' behavior tends to be directed by their relationships in this steady, enduring social system—the Guamanian extended family. When they had become participants in relationships and were appreciating the warmth and caring, they began to sense the responsibilities and obligations that are

57

inherent in this type of system. People are important; sharing is important; responsibility is important. In the integration seminar, new meanings were grasped in the context of the culture. For example, they saw that feelings of shame ("I'm shame") are part of the pattern in which each individual determines his relation to the group and that it is within this context that Guamanians set personal goals—as contrasted, for instance, with goals set by or for Americans, such as independence, achievement, and "success."

Initially the students functioned in a highly ambiguous situation as they involved themselves in developing friendships with Guamanians. They were acutely aware of being outsiders: "This is an inside-outside culture; if you are outside you are outside." They had no "person" or "channel" to help them become insiders. One student said:

> Though I can . . . recall the deep frustration I felt at being an outsider—
> deeper than anything I have ever experienced before—I would still not
> trade that experience for anything. It opened my eyes in a way that I
> doubt would ever have happened had I stayed in my own culture.

Although the students knew intellectually that they would have some failures, still, when they took the initiative with Guamanians, the emotional risk was very great. They felt shy or panicky and could not always bring themselves to act. They, of course, did experience some rejections, and they learned from them.

Comparatively speaking, developing instrumental or professional relationships carries little risk. A failure can always be rationalized: that the person/family was "not ready" or "did not want assistance" and so on. One of the objectives of the project, however, was to help students develop different skills in a variety of interactions and relationships.

We tend to assume that we can develop relationships just by being ourselves, by being frank and open and friendly. The students learned that this is not so. Our behavior may not be compatible with the cultural systems of others. In trying to behave like Guamanians, the students experienced what they called "being nothing," "sacrificing oneself," and "learning to wait." They agreed that: "You cannot be yourself and react as yourself. You have to suspend your own self, suspend your judgment, suspend your likes and dislikes so that at least you can open yourself to observe and absorb."

Some were surprised that they could and did develop meaningful relationships in a relatively short time—a tribute to the Guamanians as well as to the students. By the end of their stay in Guam, most had established warm relationships with Guamanians and found them highly rewarding;

"I feel at home; I feel as though I am an insider; I feel accepted." One student wrote:

> It was fun all working together in the preparation for the dedication. I feel so much a member of the village and responsible for the success of the celebration that I found myself responding to a request of the villagers to do certain things for the guests. It made me aware of how much a part of the village I have become.

This inner growth should not be taken as over-identifying with Guamanian culture.

As they came to appreciate Guamanians and to enjoy their friendship, students became increasingly aware of their own cultural ways or systems in contrast. Some tended to think the extended family system gave each child more attention and a greater sense of security than our nuclear family system. This led to exploration: Why have we in the United States developed T-groups, encounter groups, and so on? Why do we seem to have relatively few warm, sharing, natural friendships? Do our goals of individualism, independence, and achievement—which are different from Guamanian goals—lead to a lot of lonely, left-out people? What would it be like to live among people whom one really knows and cares about? At the same time, one said: "This system [Guamanian] does not allow as many choices as I am accustomed to and have learned to like." Another said: "Behavior in this type of relationship system makes me stop to think what it means in a broad context." The students thought that in the United States the priority that is given to scheduled goals may result in a lower priority on developing relationships, except those which are instrumental. They asked: "What changes, if any, will modernization bring in the Guamanian relationship system—and thus in all systems of the culture?"

During the integration seminar, discussion of the notion of inside-outside cultural groups brought out the fact that being totally inside a cultural group or subgroup means that one loses out on some things because one does not perceive what is happening outside. This illustrates the narrowing or blinding effect of monoculturalism.

Miscommunication and misunderstanding occurred not only because the students did not know the different time and relationship cues but also because they did not know the communication cues—either verbal or nonverbal. Indirect communication used by Guamanians—the opposite of our direct confrontation approach—left the students puzzled and uncertain. They recognized that Guamanians do not like to say no; they do not like to be turned down; they do not like confrontation and will avoid being in positions where any of these things can happen. For example, students usually did not receive direct answers to direct questions. In the integration seminar, as they reviewed their experiences in Guam, they saw indirect communication as an integral factor in maintaining smooth interpersonal relationships—an important Guamanian value. Since they did not know the cues of indirect communication they could not follow the direction and feeling tone of the conversations and did not know whether decisions or changes in plans had occurred. Asian-American students had less frustration with indirect communication. Others agreed generally that they were more comfortable with direct communication, confrontation, and expression of dissenting views.

In the same way, they could not read the cues of the nonverbal system of communication, a system likely to be more important than the spoken word. Insiders know automatically what the nonverbal messages are. Outsiders have difficulty and picking up a few of the more obvious cues does not help much. This system has to be learned in the total cultural context. Often the students were puzzled: "How can we know the difference between what is said and what is meant?" Or, "My two friends understood each other but I did not know what messages they were sending and receiving and was uncomfortable."

Illustrations of learning in three of the other culture's systems—time, interpersonal relationships, and communication—have been used to show the development of the students' capacities to find their way into a new culture. They had learned what it was they needed to learn, why they needed to learn it, and how to learn it. As one student said: "Learning of this kind is more than learning a culture; it is learning to learn." They now had developed an active understanding that the various systems of a culture are woven into patterns that differentiate one cultural group from another. A second student pointed out: "This is learning what differences as well as similarities mean; it is learning that there are different ways to perceive the world."

Readers may ask, "What is so great about that?" Just this: the students moved from being insiders in their own culture to being outsiders in another and then to becoming insiders in the other culture; in doing so their cultural self-awareness increased, as did their ability to evaluate their own culture in a new frame of reference, yet they maintained their identity with it. That is the process of becoming bicultural.

IMPLEMENTING THE DESIGN FOR CROSS-CULTURAL LEARNING

OVERVIEW

The Students

Ideally the program should be planned for small groups of students, but can be adapted to larger numbers. For the field seminar a group of 20–25 should be divided into smaller groups of five to seven students.

Selection of a Site

As explained in Chapter IV, two of the underlying assumptions of the program are that (1) the culture selected for the field experience should be very different from that of the students so the contrasts are sharp and students will experience some degree of culture shock; and (2) the site should be at sufficient geographical distance so that students have no recourse to family and friends.

Because language can be a barrier in the style of learning desired in the program, we selected cultures in which a different language is the native tongue but English is a second language—at least for a sizeable proportion of the people. If the program is going to reach the widest possible student audience, language proficiency cannot be a fixed requirement. Of course, when possible, the conduct of the program in a non-English speaking culture will enrich and intensify the experience.

Pre-planning

Careful pre-planning is needed at the site of the field experience to determine with appropriate community officials, whether urban or rural, their willingness (1) to have students enter their communities as learners (not as researchers or for any other purpose except that of getting to know the people); and (2) to sanction the project and give the support that accompanies sanction.

Depending on the culture, this may involve a more or less formal written agreement. A plan for students to be introduced into the various villages/communities is essential. The ways of introducing them may vary from the formal, such as being introduced at a special school program (*e.g.*, graduation exercises), to the informal, such as attending a community festival, visiting a village development program, etc.—but all with the intent of giving approval, making the students visible, and increasing their opportunities to meet people.

Student Living Arrangements

Arranging for student living is a part of the pre-planning operation, and, in our view, should be a joint project with local officials and others in the culture involved. Two forms of housing, dormitories and local families, have proven successful to varying degrees, depending on both the student's and the host's cultures. In some cases, living as a guest with a family worked out well, but in others it proved problematic. Two Hong Kong Chinese groups lived with families in the Philippines in suburban and rural communities, paying an agreed upon fee for room and board. In some instances this latter plan worked very well. Students thought it worked best with lower income and rural families from whom they believed they learned a great deal because the families were open and sharing in their attitudes and at the same time left students free to explore and discover the total community or village. In some instances students expended considerable time and energy in overcoming guest status or resisting being overprotected by the family. Some recorded that at times it was not easy to establish a role within the family or to go out to explore the community or develop relationships with other families. There were exceptions of course.

Coming to understand family relationships is a part of culture learning. For the Hong Kong Chinese students, family living has implications of obligations to the family; for American students, being accustomed to independence, a family situation may be experienced as confining. If a student decides to follow his independent inclination, he may never see what he is doing to the family.

If family homestays are used, the instructor needs to be sensitive in the early sessions of the field seminar to how relationships are developing with the family and to help students translate problems into learning.

Our preference, from experience, is a dormitory-style living arrangement in a university dormitory, if available, or in some other dormitory-style accommodations that will allow students full freedom to move about in the community. For American students in Guam, living in a university dormitory provided a variety of unexpected experiences, pleasant and unpleasant, and was a good plan. One Hong Kong Chinese group of students had a good experience in accommodations comparable to a dormitory at the edge of an old Chinese sea village.

We believe that five to seven is the maximum number of students to be housed together; thus, a group of 20–25 students can be accommodated in four or five locations. The dormitory-style plan requires students to become sensitive to one another, find easy ways of interacting and reach an appreciation of themselves as a group as well as individuals. Students also have the opportunity to interact or even to share a room with local students. Students should be encouraged to spend a weekend or some days, if invited, visiting a family with whom they have developed a close relationship, which we found students eager to do.

Faculty

A minimum of two faculty members should be involved in the program: one to conduct the pre-field seminar and the other to accompany students to the field and conduct both the field and post-field seminars. Ideally both instructors should be involved in the post-field seminar, but involvement of the field instructor is essential. Neither instructor would be assigned full-time to the program.

Cross-cultural learning experience is a prerequisite for the faculty involved. By this, we mean that instructors should be culturally self-aware, understand the impact of culture-based perceptual sets in determining attitudes and behavior, and have a gut-level respect and appreciation for cultural differences in others.

The instructor for the pre-field seminar should be familiar with basic cultural anthropological concepts, as well as with perception theory from social psychology, and should understand how they are woven together in human experience. The instructor should also be able to draw with ease on personal cross-cultural experience for illustrations to enrich the teaching.

The field instructor should sit in on the pre-field seminar and be familiar with the theory presented there, be skilled at leading discussions and have some understanding of group process. In particular, the instructor must be able to recognize the depth of the students' frustrations during the first weeks in the field and be able to absorb their negative feelings while retaining the conviction that they will soon be rewarded with understanding. Students sense this conviction in their instructor and need it as tacit support in the early stages of the experience.

The role of the field instructor is different from that of the traditional classroom teacher. In the field the students and their personal experience are at the center of the learning process. The instructor acts as facilitator helping them organize their experiences and relate them to the cognitive framework of cross-cultural learning. The instructor should have a living arrangement similar to that of the students and be sufficiently nearby to be easily accessible to them, but not so near that they feel the instructor is looking over their shoulders.

Credit

A total of 10 hours of academic credit is suggested: three credits for the pre-field seminar; four credits for the field experience including the field seminar; and three credits for the post-field program, including the seminar and two learning summaries. The students are given an "incomplete" grade for the post-field seminar until the date of the final summary.

Institutional Commitments

The program entails an institutional commitment to the following:

1. Two regular faculty members part-time with administrative support to carry out relevant responsibilities. The assumption is that individuals who are committed to the idea of cross-cultural experiential learning and who meet necessary qualifications will be available from among regular faculty, thus requiring minimal new budgetary allocations.

2. Assignment of regular academic credit for each of the three seminars to be cross-referenced in catalogs of the professional schools and the departments of the various disciplines. The assumption is that the program will be recognized by an increasing number of deans and directors as a valuable part of the educational program in various disciplines and professions. The 10 credits suggested can be used as an elective sequence by students or be integrated appropriately as a component of existing curricula.

THE PRE-FIELD SEMINAR

Learning Objectives

Students are expected to (1) demonstrate a consistent attitude of positive learning by contributing to class discussion from their own ideas and previous learning experience and by participating in various special learning activities; (2) become familiar with the theoretical knowledge from cultural anthropology and social psychology that is pertinent to the program; (3) demonstrate an involvement in "knowing" on an affective level by application of new theoretical knowledge in a series of short paper assignments and a final term paper; and (4) indicate at least at a superficial level an understanding of the learning objectives of the program.

The bases for grading in this seminar are: (1) class participation; (2) short assignments; and (3) a final paper. Students will report in the final paper what discoveries they have made about their perceptions and behavior that had heretofore been at the non-conscious level and analyze them in terms of cultural and subcultural influences, applying theoretical knowledge acquired in the course.

Outline of the Seminar

The seminar meets once a week for two hours for a term. It may be divided roughly into five parts:

1. Introduction: culture
2. Selective Perception: the basic theoretical foundation of the course to which succeeding topics constantly refer
3. Monoculturalism: a review of the limiting effects of culture on the way people perceive, think, and behave
4. Cross-Cultural Learning: the process of overcoming the limitation of being monocultural by living in another culture and experiencing concommitant personal growth
5. Field Orientation

Parts 1 and 5 are primarily orientation sessions. Part 1 is orientation to the objectives of the program, the objectives of the seminar, and introduction to the concept of culture as used in the seminar. Part 5 is orientation to the field experience. Parts 2 and 3 are devoted to theory while Part 4 is a discussion of cross-cultural learning.

Although the major topics in Parts 2 and 3 logically follow one another, the related topics need not have a fixed order. For instance, "culture" is discussed in the first session, but the culture-language-communication relationship might be included in discussion of American culture in relation to being monocultural.

The seminar should take a minimum of ten weeks, but for a longer term, in-and-out-of-class activities and discussion time might be increased.

Classroom Activities and Outside Assignments

Visual Perception: A 20-minute educational film developed by the National Science Foundation[48] helps students realize how perception can distort reality. The film shows the strength of our habits of perceptual inference which are formed by past experience and which are difficult to break, even with conscious effort. This is particularly the case with the Ames Trapezoid in the film. The trapezoid, which is rotating in complete circles, is perceived as a rectangular window oscillating back and forth. Even with aids to perceive the rotation, the illusion of oscillation tends to persist. The fact that some people in Africa, living in an environment where no rectangular windows are to be found, do not see the illusion (Allport and Pettigrew, 1957) should be convincing evidence of environmental (both cultural and physical) influence on perceptual habits.

Symbol Perception Test: Niyekawa devised this test to demonstrate selective perception. It consists of colored symbols on slides projected on a screen tachistoscopically or in rapid succession by a carousel projector. Forty slides, with one symbol per slide, were carefully selected from among a pool of 120 to meet the following criteria: (1) symbols some of which are more easily recognized by women, and others by men—such as trademarks of cosmetics, motorcycles, etc., which show sex differences; (2) symbols more familiar to certain ethnic groups, such as trademarks of ethnic food items; (3) symbols found only in particular regions, states, or cities in the U.S., such as those for telephone companies, subways, or supermarket chains; (4) symbols of airlines, long distance buses, trains, hotel chains, cars, clothing manufacturers, chinaware, etc., to show difference in interest and experience; (5) some local symbols everybody can recognize; and (6) symbols associated with the country or location to which the students are headed. Care is taken to include a range of colors, sizes, shapes, and varying degrees of complexity in design, and to include a number of symbols which are similar in shape or design to each other. After the rapid presentation of the 40 slides, students are given a recogni-

---

[48]The film *Visual Perception* was made by Dr. Hadley Cantril of Princeton University in 1959. It is distributed by Educational Testing Service, Audio Visual Division, and is available from major university and other audio-visual collections around the country.

tion test booklet consisting of several sheets containing the entire set of 120 symbols in black and white. They are to circle those they think they saw. Since it is impossible for anyone to recognize all the 40 symbols correctly, selectivity in perception and memory based on each individual's background and interest becomes evident. The role of labeling will also be noticed as an aid in memory. An exciting discussion usually follows the test.

Listening in Silence: This is an exercise in auditory perception. Everyone remains silent for two or three minutes, then jots down all the stimuli he/she has noted during this time. When the results are put on the blackboard, the students can recognize, with guidance, the concept of perceptual difference and how it limits one's views.

Sudden Intruder: In the midst of a lecture someone enters the classroom to deliver a message to the instructor. This intrusion is pre-arranged, but to the students it appears to be unexpected and irrelevant. To make sure that the students take notice, the messenger might drop a book when handing the message to the instructor. The messenger departs. Half an hour or so later, the instructor asks the students to write down a description of the messenger, which is followed by class discussion. The students are thus asked to respond to an ambiguous stimulus. Examples of selective perception including labeling (*i.e.*, "awkward" in dropping the book), categorizing and stereotyping, are relatively easy to draw from the descriptions.

Practice in Field Observation: Students pair off in two's to observe a small group of two or three people for 15 to 20 minutes in a park, shopping center, bus station, and so on. Without any discussion between them, either during or after the observation, each writes his/her interpretations of the observation. Copies of these paired observations are distributed to all students for comparison and for discussion in the subsequent class session. The observations reveal both affective and cognitive dimensions as the students make interpretations and judgments. Even in the choice of words in describing the same people and events, selective perception is revealed. This exercise has a powerful impact in helping students become conscious of their own perceptual processes.

"Who Am I?" Test: This five- to ten-minute test requires students to jot down on a piece of paper how they would describe themselves or what they are, such as student, or student at X University, Italian-American, Texan, liberal, conservationist, etc., listed in the order they come to mind. Another way to do this is to list on the left half of the paper, "What I Am" and on the right half, "What I Am Not." Discussion of the two lists will reveal negative stereotypes held.

Telephone Caller: This is an assignment which is effective in making students aware of the automatic manner in which they judge and assess people. It involves taking a message over the phone and assessing the caller by guessing age, sex, educational level, geographical background, etc. using only the voice and speech patterns as clues. Discussion enables students to recognize how automatically they make judgments and engage in stereotyping.

BaFa BaFa: In this simulation of the experience of entering another culture, ten to forty participants are divided into two groups and learn differrent sets of "cultural" behaviors. Visits back and forth simulate cross-cultural interaction as each group tries to decipher the meaning of the behavior of the other. Simulations are an enjoyable way to introduce people to basic concepts of cultural and perceptual difference and cross-cultural interaction and analysis. (Published by Simile II, Box 910, Del Mar, CA 92014.)

Many useful activities have been developed for cross-cultural learning. These can be found in: *Intercultural Sourcebook*, Hoopes and Ventura, 1979; *Beyond Experience*, Batchelder and Warner, 1977; *Overview of Intercultural Education, Training and Research, Vol. II, Education and Training*, Hoopes, Pedersen, and Renwick, 1978; *Developing Intercultural Awareness*, Kohls, 1982; and *Survival Kit for Overseas Living*, Kohls, revised edition 1984.

Selected Reading Assignments for Each Topic

Selective Perception
Attneave, F. "Multistability in Perception," *Scientific American*, 1971, V. 225, 6 (Dec.), pp. 62–71.
Bruner J. S. "Social Psychology and Perception." In E. E. Maccoby, T. M. Newcomb, and E. L. Hartley (Eds.) *Readings in Social Psychology*. New York: Hold, Rinehart & Winston, 1958, pp. 85–94.
Combs, A. W. "Intelligence From a Perceptual Point of View." *Journal of Abnormal and Social Psychology*, 1952, V. 47, pp. 662–73.

Labeling and Categorization
Brown, R. W. "Language and Categories." In J. S. Bruner, J. J. Goodnow, and G. A. Austin. *A Study of Thinking*. New York: John Wiley, 1956, pp. 247–312.
Hallowell, A. I. "Cultural Factors in the Structuralization of Perception." In L. A. Samovar and R. E. Porter (Eds.) *Intercultural Communication: A Reader*. Belmont, CA: Wadsworth, 1972, pp. 49–68.
Leeper, R. "An Experiment with Ambiguous Figures." In D. E. Dulany Jr., R. L. DeValois, D. C. Beardslee, & M. R. Winterbottom. *Contributions to Modern Psychology*. New York: Oxford University Press, 1963, pp. 123–34.

Stereotyping
Lambert, W. E. *et al.* "Evaluation Reactions to Spoken Languages." *Journal of Abnormal and Social Psychology*, 1960, V. 60, pp. 44–51.

Wedge, B. "Nationality and Social Perception." In L. A. Samovar and R. E. Porter (Eds.) *Intercultural Communication: A Reader.* Belmont, CA: Wadsworth, 1972, pp. 69–75.

Culture, Language and Communication
Kluckhohn, C. "The Gift of Tongues." In L. A. Samovar and R. E. Porter (Eds.) *Intercultural Communication: A Reader.* Belmont, CA: Wadsworth, 1972, pp. 104–14.
Porter, R. E. "An Overview of Intercultural Communication." In L. A. Samovar and R. E. Porter (Eds.) *Intercultural Communication: A Reader.* Belmont, CA: Wadsworth, 1972, pp. 3–18.

American Culture
Barnhurst, Kevin G. "The Lumpen Middle Class." *The American Scholar,* 1982, V. 51, 3, pp. 369–78.
Lederer, W. J. and Eugene Burdick. *The Ugly American.* New York: W. W. Norton & Co., 1958.
Miner, H. "Body Ritual among the Nacirema." *American Anthropologist,* 1956, V. 38, 3, pp. 503–7.
Stewart, E. C. and Milton Bennett. *American Cultural Patterns: A Cross-Cultural Perspective.* Yarmouth, ME: Intercultural Press, 1986.

Cultural Bias and Cultural Delimitation
Cole, M. and S. Scribner. *Culture and Thought.* New York: John Wiley & Sons, 1974.
Detweiler, R. A. "Intercultural Interaction and the Categorization Process: A Conceptual Analysis and Behavioral Outcome." *International Journal of Intercultural Relations,* 1980, V. 4, pp. 275–93.

Personal Growth
Otto, H. A. "New Light on Human Potential." In A. Arkoff (Ed.) *Psychology and Personal Growth.* Boston, London, Sydney: Allyn and Bacon, 1975, pp. 299–306.
Jourard, S. M. "Growing Experience and the Experience of Growth." In A. Arkoff (Ed.) *Psychology and Personal Growth.* Boston, London, Sydney: Allyn and Bacon, 1975, pp. 307–15.

Field Methodology
Bennett, J. "Transition Shock: Putting Culture Shock in Perspective." *International and Intercultural Communication Annual,* V. 3, 1979, pp. 45–52.

FIELD EXPERIENCE

Learning Objectives and Field Design

Stated explicitly, the behavioral objectives for the field learning experience are (1) to understand the values, assumptions, attitudes, and behaviors which constitute the cultural framework of the host society, to develop an empathic sense of the way it works for the people, to appreciate and respect the validity of different values and ways of life, and to develop an approach to learning a culture that is applicable to learning other cultures; and (2) to experience personal growth by (a) developing an awareness of one's own values and culturally determined behaviors; (b) learning to form and maintain sincere friendships with a variety of people in the host culture; (c) developing the ability to appreciate cultural differences; and (d) learning to evaluate oneself in relation to cross-cultural situations, *i.e.* assessing cross-cultural competence.

In our experience, a two-month period is the minimum time required for students to attain the learning objectives. The field experience is graded on the extent to which students meet the learning objectives as reflected in their daily journal and participation in the seminar.

The field design includes three explicit types of learning activities: (1) developing friendships, (2) a daily journal, and (3) a field seminar.

Developing Friendships

Developing friendships with people of the host culture is in itself very demanding. "I am an outsider," laments the newly arrived student. The combination of culture shock, lack of a specific role and other uncertainties require students to depend heavily on their own inner resources at a time when their customary behaviors do not serve them well. The design builds in certain psychological and environmental supports that serve a sustaining function, particularly in the early period.

Daily Journal

In their journals, students are requested to record their observations, reactions, experiences, frustrations and feelings, problems, ideas and questions, but for the first several weeks to try limiting themselves to describing what has happened rather than interpreting or categorizing it. This helps them avoid imposing culture-bound judgments too quickly on their experiences before they can discover the meaning and patterns of the other culture.

The stipulation "to describe" is important. The customary behavior in one's own culture is to interpret and categorize; we do it automatically and may not recognize at first that we are still doing it even when it is no longer relevant.

The journal is, then, an integral part of the field experience, providing students with the opportunity to look both inward and outward in a process of reflection. As one student noted perceptively, "It takes me a couple of days sometimes to turn some of my experiences into reflections."

Field Seminar

The seminar which meets once a week for three hours (more if students wish, and sometimes they do) to integrate affective with cognitive learning. It flags the affective learning while it is occurring and provides an opportunity to:

- release feelings, frustrations, misunderstandings, uncertainties into the public forum of the group—outside the self, but in a safe place
- examine ideas and questions in the context of peer give-and-take
- relate experiences to the concepts learned in the pre-field seminar
- fit the fragments of their experiences into the pattern of the host culture.

The faculty member's role is that of a facilitator, encouraging the students to probe more deeply into the meaning of their experiences. Thus, his or her responsibility is to:

- create an atmosphere safe for spontaneous expression of feelings
- help students to explore, question and experiment
- facilitate the translation of immediate experiences into meanings which fit the cognitive framework of cross-cultural learning.

As Douglas Steere reports Martin Buber saying: "The greatest thing . . . that any person can do for another is to confirm the deepest thing he has within him."[49] That is what the faculty member must do in the field learning situation.

IMPLEMENTATION

In order to implement the design, the following conditions need to be met:

1. Selection of a learning site that creates (a) cultural distance and (b) geographical distance, to minimize reinforcement of the students' own culture.

2. Living arrangements in a dormitory or with local families, as discussed above. Students should know before departure from home the exact financial arrangements and their responsibility for budgeting.

3. Arrangements and procedures for the sanction and introduction of

---

[49]Steere, 1976, 16–17.

students into the setting of the other culture to be developed jointly with appropriate authorities/agencies in that culture.

4. Access provided for the students, in the initial period, to some individuals in the other culture (agency personnel, etc.) who can serve as anchors but who will leave the students free to find their own learning experiences.

5. Proximity and availability of the accompanying faculty member who will have living quarters relatively similar to those of the students.

To facilitate acceptance by the members of the community, authorities must sanction the presence of students and publicly welcome them.

The first community activity for students after their arrival is a visit to the Village Commissioner/Head Committee/Mayor and any other supporting agencies. The faculty member should accompany the students on this visit. Continuity and a sense of stability in the program are important.

Sometimes the authorities or agencies use the visit simply to affirm the plan, give some information (even advice) about the locale and the people, ask a question or two, welcome the students to the community, and outline briefly any basic regulations that govern the community. Sometimes they evidence a strong interest (and may even become involved with students throughout their stay) and suggest various people and institutions with whom the students might like to become acquainted. At other times authorities may ask the students why they have come, even though it has already been explained to them.

Officials find it hard to believe that students have no instrumental role and want only to learn the culture from their relationships with the people. This type of learning tends to elude simple explanation. Nor is it easy for students to explain—in part because their own commitment is still in the "idea" stage. They usually find the support of the faculty member reassuring, and, interestingly enough, they seem, as they struggle to articulate it, to grasp the significance of this type of learning almost for the first time in its true meaning. Occasionally an official will want to "set up" a program for students. When and if this occurs, it becomes, in itself, a problem-solving experience for students.

This first meeting with the community officials proves to have considerably more significance to students than may be attributed to it initially. It gives sanction directly to them; at the same time, they recognize that they are outsiders. Students can be expected throughout the entire period to refer back to this meeting and to interpret and reinterpret the meaning of what went on. If the official agreement calls for students to live with families, the families arrange for introductions at the local level. Without these visits and introductions, the students may be non-persons in the culture.

Arrangements should be made, in the pre-planning period, for various agency personnel to serve as anchors in the beginning days as students seek to learn about communities, geography, transportation, schools, etc. The anchor people can provide information (sometimes conflicting, of course) that helps students get a "handle" on their explorations.

POST-FIELD PROGRAM

The post-field program consists of two learning summaries and a seminar and is assigned three academic credits. Students are graded on the basis of their participation in the seminar, a final essay test and the quality of the learning summaries.

Learning Objectives

The learning objectives of the post-field program call for the students to demonstrate the ability to:

- organize their field learning into a systematic whole, connecting its parts and relating it to the conceptual framework provided in the pre-field seminar
- develop facility in the use of theoretical and experiential learning, especially in making cross-cultural learning a continuing process
- identify changes within themselves which have resulted from the learning.

First Summary

The intervening month between the end of the field experience and the submission of the first summary gives time for reflection. Students are asked to develop the summary in their own way but to include in it both negative and positive aspects. Writing this summary is intended to help them to see and formulate ideas about their experiences as a whole and identify changes within themselves.

Seminar

The post-field seminar is a continuation of the field seminar except that the students are not coping with the practical problems and pressures of the field; their defenses are lower, and they feel freer to examine their learning objectively. Ideally the seminar begins within two or three weeks after the students have written the first summary and serves to help them continue learning and sustain their personal growth.

The opening session is a general discussion among the students and instructor of their experiences and reactions on re-entering the home culture as well as their suggestions and ideas about what they would do differently if they were to repeat the cross-cultural learning experience. The next several sessions are devoted to study of a theoretical framework of culture. The reader will recall that, although there is discussion of culture in the pre-field seminar, students are at that time given no structural framework for analyzing culture. This omission is deliberate in order to keep their minds as clear as possible for simple observation and description. They are ready now, however, for theory.

As noted earlier, we like to use the framework provided by Edward Hall in *The Silent Language*. Hall's schema provides a comprehensive conceptual design based on the notion that culture is communication and communication is culture. According to Hall, the substance of communication, as the term is used here, consists of the messages relayed through a "primary message system" consisting of the broad spectrum of human activity occurring principally in ten areas: interaction, association, subsistence, bisexuality, territoriality, temporality, learning, play, defense, and exploitation. Further, these message systems occur on three different levels—the formal (rights and wrongs of the society; cultural norms), the informal (unconscious habits and behaviors), and the technical (consciously learned knowledge).

The three levels are present at all times in a person's behavior but one will dominate in any given situation. When formal patterns of behavior are threatened, as in learning another culture, people may cling tenaciously to perceptions they already hold, not realizing that they are reacting on the wrong level. Unless the meaning of the formal and informal level is understood and taken into account, genuine communication will be difficult. Misunderstanding is likely because people may be trying unknowingly to communicate on two different levels.

Students can begin their study with any aspect of Hall's system with which they feel comfortable and then move on to others. For example, if they choose to begin with "association," in thinking about community structure, they might then move with ease to "interaction" at the level of communication or to "learning" relative to how children are taught by parents, or to space relationships, etc. The interconnectedness of the system in actual behavioral situations becomes apparent rather quickly. Students may also need help in grasping the concept of the three levels of culture.

Once they begin to understand how the framework can be used, the next several seminar sessions are devoted to analyzing their field learn-ing—with the help of their journals, memory recall, tape-recorded materi-al from the field seminar, and their first summaries, thus creating a living model of the culture as they now see it. For example, the role and function of various people in the Guam community structure (association system) was a good place to begin to see how the role attributed to (and carried by) the Commissioner tended to establish (1) relationships in the total commu-nity, (2) expectations of families and individuals, (3) other role relation-ships in the community, (4) the value placed on education, and so on. The Commissioner also outlined the focus of community social life and set the pattern for young people's recreation. To grasp how the "levels" concept applied, it was noted that people who worked for the government (West-ern-style operation) arrived at and left work punctually (clock time). At home and in social situations these same people operated on "Guamanian time." Using the "levels" concept, students recognized that these people were operating on the technical level with respect to work and on the formal level in social situations and relationships.

Students soon feel free to move into examining some of their own relationships and experiences in the field. For instance, the students in Guam had arranged an evening picnic with song and story to which boys and girls were invited together. However, only a few Guamanian young people came (a demonstration of respect), and those who did stayed only briefly. Re-examining this experience in the context of the analytical framework, students could see that they were operating on the technical level (this would be an opportunity for boys and girls to enjoy being together) while the Guamanian young people were operating on a formal level and could not violate their cultural norms (custom does not sanction such group activities with boys and girls together). Since the American and Guamanian young people were, without being aware of it, trying to communicate on two different levels, genuine communication did not occur. This small incident, seen in a broad perspective is, of course, what happens frequently in cross-cultural communication situations.

In handling the study of legends, instructors may need to do a bit of research in order to provide students a little background on their nature and function.

Legends are unverifiable stories, popularly accepted as historical, which are handed down by tradition and which embody the basic beliefs, values and accepted ways of a culture. In some Pacific and Asian cultures many important legends (in prose and poetry) reveal an attitude of reverence for and harmony with nature. In other cultures, Europe, for example, legends (in prose, poetry, and opera) reflect the value placed on conquering armies (often fighting for Christianity), exploitation of nature, the role of men, heroic deeds, etc. Many American legends extol the hero who conquers all obstacles to achieve and succeed. Legends often teach obedience and warn against disobedience (violating customs or taboos) or show how sharing is rewarded and greed punished. Legends reflect what people regard as "good" (personified often as the beautiful, loving princess) and imply or state what is considered evil. The power of evil is feared and is often personified as the devil, Satan, trolls, giants, ogres, and so on. Legends about death in some cultures portray the celebration of life, making death a joyful occasion for the deceased (though the living may mourn). In other cultures, careful attention is given to following customs with care in order to avoid having the dead come back as evil spirits, which evidences fear of the unknown and also of what is sometimes referred to as "unfinished business," the nasty things the dead person did to others and which have not been recompensed.

In Europe legends that are used by the clergy in sermons to portray the positive value of Christianity which regularly triumphs over the negative power of Satan. Sometimes legends provide the basis for attitudes about work and play—Western legends tend to praise work as a duty and regard play, like sex, as almost sinful, while Pacific legends reflect an intermingling and enjoyment of both work and play.

Thus, the examination of selected legends of a culture provides for students another source in culture learning. This exploration calls for understanding the symbolism of the legend in the cultural context and then examining it within Hall's framework of message systems to ascertain which of the culture's values and customs are relevant. One legend is not likely, of course, to reflect values across the whole range of "message systems," but in the process of analysis the students discover how values permeate behavior in several systems and learn a lesson in the consistency of culture.

In addition to class participation in the seminar, students are given an essay test at the end of the term that presents a hypothetical cross-cultural problem situation which the students are asked to analyze, using their cognitive and experiential learning, and for which they must recommend a solution.

The Final Summary

In their final summary, students are asked to evaluate the changes that have occurred in themselves which appear to be relatively permanent and to comment on changes which they thought had taken place but which proved to be transient. They are also asked to describe how their learning is reflected in their daily living.

STAGES OF LEARNING IN THE FIELD EXPERIENCE: EXAMPLES FROM STUDENT RESPONSES

In order to give the reader a more concrete idea of just how students respond to the field experience and how the learning progresses, we offer here examples from the Guam program. They include excerpts from the journals and commentary on the field seminar organized according to the stages of learning as defined in Chapter IV. Some of the reactions, classified as "cultural observations," are quoted within the context of Hall's message system framework.

Please note that both the authors and the students are aware that the comments, ideas, and formulations of the students about their experiences in Guam and about the culture of Guam may be inaccurate or reflect misunderstandings. The important thing is that they reveal the process of learning experienced by the students.

FIRST STAGE: DISORGANIZATION

Journals

The journals were primarily descriptive during this period, but they also reflected a range of reactions which largely fall into categories such as physical discomfort, personal discomfort, interpersonal relations, reactions to the new culture, and cultural observations.

Physical Discomfort. The emotional importance to Westerners of physical

77

comfort is evident in the first reactions of students to a different environment.

> There is no hot water, no keys for the rooms, and the bathrooms are not clean, but the thing that really bothers me is the washer being out of order. The rest seems minor tonight, but little things can grow on you.

> I am repulsed by the condition of the washrooms . . . and some of our rooms need much cleaning. Red ants are everywhere, walls, floor, ceiling. Can I get used to all the bugs and ants?

Annoyance with lack of services to which they were accustomed was noted:

> The telephone system is a nuisance; it is almost nonexistent. There is no mail pick-up time posted on any mail boxes on campus; the postal service on campus is sporadic and, unbelievably, the main Guam post office ran out of stamps!

A few students found the food "hot and spicy" and had "to wash it down with water." Another said, "I distrust the food and water; I'm sure I'm going to be sick." One student noted enjoyment of a food that was familiar: "Delicious food at the 'X' closing program, soft chocolate-flavored rice."

Personal Discomfort. During this period some students wrote of a sense of internal discomfort that appeared to be related to their situation.

> Tired, and I am not comfortable. I hope this feeling will diminish.

> Had lunch at P.'s, mostly "haoles" [statesiders]. This is the first time in several days that I have felt comfortable and certain of what I was doing.

Others identified sources of discomfort:

> The first week's seminar was loose and I think we didn't say what we are feeling.

> I am frustrated because I can't put things together to make patterns. We are invited to many fiestas and celebrations but I don't yet see these as valuable since we talk mostly among ourselves.

Several students experienced ethnic discomfort:

> I felt uneasy when A. told T. I am Japanese. I thought there was some negative feeling in his tone of voice, and I have never felt so uneasy regarding my ethnic background.

At the shopping center I [a Caucasion] was conscious of looking different from most people. Few people smiled, and I felt they see me as an outsider who might be trying to impose stress-provoking aspects of my culture.

I tried to get a salt shaker so I could be sprinkled with salt, the Japanese way, to keep the dead spirits away after viewing the funeral. This may sound strange but this was passed down by my parents and I do not choose to challenge the tradition.

Journal entries that involve interactions reflect the pervasiveness of discomfort arising from not knowing how to behave and not understanding meanings, as well as from taking risks and finding they have made mistakes:

I am uncomfortable because I can't understand, I'm not sure about things and can't communicate effectively. Very frustrating.

It is difficult for us to interact with others because we tend to sit together and stay together as a group.

We made a mistake by going to the reception at K's. The invitation was not really for us and we missed the cues. I don't understand the cues about invitations. I think we were considered outsiders at the J. party.

At the fiesta I walked to the back where two girls from our group were talking to a group of men. The Guamanian women looked at me as I passed and I became uncomfortable. I think we shouldn't have been there.

I feel quite panicky about talking with people. In spite of knowing that I must make the first move I can't do it right now even when I have good openings. Worries me.

Putting the Cultural Pieces Together. From time to time the students noted that they had only bits and pieces and could make nothing from the fragments. In summing up at the end of the second week, one student wrote:

I think I am beginning to understand a little of Guamanian culture. Sometimes I am too tired to be observant. Never knew it could take so much energy. May already be taking some things for granted. Have to watch this. Find I am writing less of what I observe and becoming more reflective. Is this a feature of beginning to understand or a blasé attitude? My observations are becoming less haphazard. It takes a couple of days to turn my observations into useful reflections.

The purpose of our being here fell into place for me today. Now I feel a definite direction in our presence and involvement (second week).

Cultural Observations. Observations, ideas, and questions about Guamanian culture were somewhat fragmentary but they ranged across quite a number of Hall's primary message systems and can be so organized. The students did not make such an organization and the various topics were separate from each other. They were not seen as parts of a larger whole and some were stated simply as contrasts to their own cultural frame of reference.

Toward the end of the two-week period, comments like these were common:

At this point there seems to be no one Guamanian way.

From talking with B. we began to get a feel for the variations and complexities of the culture.

Time, Appointments. Some students were more observant in their reaction to differences in the Guamanian concept of time:

I don't understand why people say they will be on time and either don't come or arrive late.

What does it mean when people say yes and/or make an appointment and don't keep it? How can we pick up cues as to when a person is really going to do what he says and when not?

Maybe when people make an appointment for a certain time it is because they think it is what we want and do not consider it rude to break it, although it might be rude to refuse to make it.

Interaction/Communication. Interaction and communication overlap at times with ideas about relationships. The observations are fairly scattered and connections among the observations are not made. At the same time one notes that the students have recognized some of the more subtle aspects of Guamanian communication even though they do not understand them:

Introductions seem important for outsiders. People seem to open up and become more friendly if they know who you are and why you are here. A. said, "My people don't know you well yet. They will be friendlier when they do."

G. didn't tell me there is only one key to a room. Why? Do Guamanians not tell a person what they know he doesn't want to hear?

People seem not to take initiative in conversations. Is this part of a concept of no disagreements, no confrontations, but smooth interpersonal relationships?

I asked a woman how Guamanians say no and she didn't answer until I asked several times; then she said, "Do you mean a definite no?" Does this mean there are various ways?

I am impressed with the hospitality of people. They place high priority on giving and sharing.

Family. Students' observations and impressions about family are stated mostly as contrasts with their own concepts of family.

Children generally seem to be a joy rather than a burden. People like large families and children appear to get a great deal of attention, not all of it from the mother, but from many family members.

Guamanians show respect for older people, kiss the hand, and respect the wisdom of years. They enjoy older people and care for them. A Sunday visit to the grandparents' home is fun. Children are enjoyed and shared with all the family.

The mother appears to discipline and punish children except for a very serious situation and then she may ask the father's help. Children are punished physically more often than in the United States. Some Guamanians say "statesiders do not understand the Guamanian method of punishment but it is good."

Parents seem to be more permissive than in the U.S. with respect to noisy children; they may make a verbal reprimand but if the behavior is not serious, it continues and the mother lets it go. Children appear to be punished, however, for disobedience.

Youth and Dating. Students became aware early of a different type of parental practice with respect to dating. A visit to Youth Hall (a facility for young people with behavior problems) added to their interest:

How do young people meet each other and decide they want to marry? School? Parties? How well do a boy and girl know each other before marriage? Some parents say there is a strict system of no dating and others say there is some dating. But what does dating mean here?

"Out of control" [a phrase used when parents ask to have a youth sent to Youth Hall] seems to mean that the youth won't obey the parents or may have run away from home. Staff at Youth Hall say the youth are mostly misdirected.

Money. Observations regarding the meaning of money bring underlying values of the new culture into perspective:

There is always much food—perhaps the tradition of abundance is more important than expense or waste.

One woman said Guamanians don't worry much about money; friends are important.

Fiestas and celebrations are important enough so that people may borrow money for them. Part of the pay check may often be put aside for this purpose.

Houses. The students were struck by the contrast between their own values and those of the Guamanian culture with regard to houses.

One can't judge economic status from the outside of a house. Money is not spent on fancy houses and furniture. What is important?

At times I am shocked. Houses are so different from my idea of homes.

Houses are usually small and unpretentious; the inside is clean and knick-knacks are used to make it attractive. Often there is no glass in the windows. The outside around the house is often messy. Many homes have no indoor plumbing.

Supernatural Beliefs. These beliefs had come into conversations from the beginning.

Although some Guamanians profess not to believe, others say "Taotao-monas[50] [spirits of ancient Chamorros] live in the woods, and many of us are careful." A number of people have made reference to taotaomonas, and despite some denials, the belief comes through from time to time.

---

[50]The taotaomonas are believed to be Chamorros who have been killed and who haunted their old land districts, not as gods or ghosts, but as men of super-human strength. They are believed to impose certain ta-boos. If a person found himself astray in a district not his own, he might be harmed by these spirits unless he asked permission to enter the district. Once on the land he dared not sing, urinate, fish, pick fruits, or hunt without permission. Belief in the taotaomonas is said to have sustained the social system of Guam in ancient days.

I was told that parents of the older generation do not swear at their children—they hold the belief that the curse might come true.

Language and Concepts. Apparently the students had forgotten that they had been told how various languages classify objects and events differently and that some languages do not make the gender distinctive in the third person singular pronoun.

Why do Guamanians use the pronouns "he" and "she" without reference to the sex of the person? Some people in Hawaii do this, too.

The concept of privacy is probably different than in the U.S. My roommate (a Guamanian) waited to move in until I came because it would be lonely in the room alone—and I am more concerned with privacy and a place to be alone.

What does the term "lazy" mean—or does it have more than one meaning? An aide spoke of someone as lazy but this man had cleared several acres of land and was growing plants and producing chickens. He just wanted to stay on the land. Is this an example of transition in culture and is one lazy who doesn't want to get involved in the cash economy? But a woman who has six children says she is "lazy" to have more.

What does shame mean? A friend said, "I would feel shame to dance out there until others are dancing."

The Field Seminar

The early sessions of the field seminar affirmed the disorganization reflected in the students' journals in this first stage of learning. The students had some concern about whether the journals were "acceptable"—thereby revealing the typical academic learning expectation. Telling them that there was no preconceived notion of what would be "acceptable" did not help, nor did a brief review of the discussion in the pre-training seminar about the journals. This rational reply did not respond to their needs for approval in relation to the journals, which was really the only area in which they could get customary assurance.

Some members used the first session mainly to discuss frustrations, *e.g.* lack of opportunity to pursue their interests independently of their relationships with the Guamanians. There was recognizable discomfort among members of the group and with the instructor. Questions were raised about the amount of time being used to get acquainted everywhere.

It seemed too long, some said, but one student quoted a Guamanian who had said, "The best way to get acquainted is to try to be introduced formally and there will be some kind of gathering when you can be welcomed officially, so to speak, or the commissioner will officially welcome you to the village. Then, when you go into the village, it is simple." It was suggested that if this point were valid, it was the approach for which to aim. One member of the group suggested that we discuss the best ways for the group to use all the journals, the best ways for the seminar to be used, and whether sharing a cultural comment might give some insights. The group agreed that each student would read his own and every other student's journal prior to each session. Some decided to exchange ideas as they were reading and come to the seminar with what had emerged from these exchanges. In this way, all would benefit from an expanded perspective, and the presentation of alternatives ideas would move them to more substantive exploration.

The next session of this group was a mixture of expressions of discomfort and frustration and expressions revealing shifts in reactions. Some students said: "We are not moving fast enough," or "I'm feeling very shy about talking with people." Sharing of feeling and discussion about talking with people was helpful.

Changes in their reactions were also revealed: "For the first time I really got involved and I had risked quite a bit"; "I like it but I don't feel as much freedom as I do at home"; "For the first time in a week I thought about the showers being cold, and I don't feel I have to get the ants off the wall, so I am making progress." The students challenged the instructor's view that they should arrive by "clock time" for appointments made with Guamanians even though they knew people would not be ready until later. They did not accept the explanation that Guamanians would expect them to observe their own cultural pattern at the same time as Guamanians would observe theirs. Several of the students reacted so strongly to time situations that the instructor asked, "How can we move beyond just being angry and fighting this? We need to express our feelings but can we move beyond and try to learn what time means to Guamanians as different from what it means in the United States?"

By the end of the second session it was clear that students felt a need to talk more openly, with no holds barred, about feelings, frustrations, discontent, plans and schedules, and so on. They asked for a special meeting.

The groping of students toward a new style of learning in an ambiguous situation in which they could not use their old style was clearly evident in the ephemeral quality of the seminar sessions.

SECOND STAGE: RE-EXAMINATION
Journals

Although personal discomforts continued, they tended to be manifested in the context of interaction with people, and the students showed some capacity to see themselves in the interchange:

> There surely is a lot I don't understand about this culture. Made another mistake because of miscommunication. When we returned to the office, lunch was not there as before, and, intending to be thoughtful, I suggested we might go to Y.'s to eat. E. seemed angry and said if I preferred the food there, to go, but there is plenty of food here. We found our lunch in the refrigerator and although I recognized my error I couldn't seem to explain why I had made the suggestion.

> Changed my approach today—not asking many questions, just looked cheerful and interested. It really worked. People seemed less threatened and came forward to talk and some initiated conversation.

> I don't know how to make small talk with Guamanians. I ask about their lives and they don't ask about me. Maybe I shouldn't ask—how do they feel about it? Maybe I should just keep quiet and see what Guamanians talk about.

> My own culture and what is important to me stands out so much more clearly in the background of another culture.

Reactions to the new culture reflected not only a desire to understand but also an ability to make finer discriminations.

> Boys at the Dairy Queen are oblivious to the long waiting line and take care of each customer as though he is the only one.

> People don't seem to mind waiting.

> Funny, Americans have to be on time even to have fun. To me time is precious. I don't like wasting it, especially if it is my fun time. This sounds strange now that I think about it.

> Maybe there are differences according to the situation. Perhaps among friends time is not so important. One of the girls said there is no word in Chamorro for "late"; no expression for "What time is it?"

Other comments illustrate how students were attempting to learn the meaning of some of the differences in the new culture:

> I asked L. whether she ever had time to be alone. She said not much, but sometimes just the family will be at home and will sit around and eat and talk together. Did L. understand what I mean? Or does she consider being with the family being alone? Is being alone valued or needed?

> Planning does not seem to work very well. Planned a hike, but it did not get organized and we couldn't go. I went to S. for a Youth Club meeting. Again, planning problems and the organizing meeting did not materialize. Is this related in any way to Guamanian concept of time?

We had been asking ourselves periodically how we seemed to the Guamanians. One indication was a question from one of the Guamanian university students at the dormitory. She didn't understand why young men and women were permitted to travel together if they were not married. She had assumed the students were all married to one another.

The Field Seminar

The discussion was less disjointed this week than previously. The group immediately began an exploration of their cultural observations and questions; the emphasis was on cognitive learning. There was some evidence of divergent thinking as they explored several possible interpretations of a cultural phenomenon which they did not yet understand and for which they could still not identify a pattern.

Significance of the Family. Several members of the group had become increasingly interested in the extended family:

> A.'s journal notes that one parent said it is the duty or responsibility of a parent to provide a house for married children. Our journals have previously suggested that parents want their married children to live at home. We haven't considered the possibility that to provide housing may be regarded as a duty or responsibility. How does this tie in with what we have said so far, that as long as children are under the parental roof (even to 50 years of age) they are not totally independent?

> There is something far different in family here than where I come from in the United States. A sense of continuity? A closely knit group almost a community? If true, it might give a clue. Perhaps it gives prestige and respect to be able to say, "I can provide for others," or say, "I am responsible for the welfare of the family." This kind of interdependence, as different from in the United States, suggests a different way of thinking about yourself, about roles, about relationships. We need to learn more about the kinship situation. People appear to get their identity through family relationships. Parents have obligations to children, children have obligations to parents, and godparents have obligations. Every-

one is obligated by blood and, in addition, because people do things for you.

Time. The concept of Guamanian time was still a puzzle and now someone put the question this way:

> The U.S. economic system depends on time and efficiency and this is what we think is "right" and "best" and it is appropriate in our system. We can't stand wasting time. In Guam, a person really waits on each customer, each gets full attention no matter how long the line, and the employee is not upset by this. Does the system and way of life here call for efficiency? If not, what does it call for as having high priority in value? Can we try to work on this?

THIRD STAGE: REORGANIZATION

Journals

One student whose attitude outwardly seemed to remain essentially negative during this period actually found the learning to be positive. Several students experienced swings of mood.

> I'm not as happy here as at home. My normal sources of rewards are missing—people I know. Here the flow of communication is more difficult. Here I relate to all people, not those I select, as at home.

A week later this same student wrote:

> The longer I am here the easier it gets. There are rewards in this culture but it takes time to learn how to get them.

Another student wrote:

> I surely feel alone in these situations when I meet a new family. I find it difficult to make conversation. Can I do it? I'm tired of not knowing the rules, not being able to read the cues.

A day or so later, the student wrote:

> The only way to have meaningful relationships is to try, to risk, and, if I am rejected, well, just to go on. I wonder how I come across to Guamanian people? I'm very aware these last several days of the closeness of the people in this village.

And yet a few days later this student wrote:

> Despite the fact that G. didn't give me a warm greeting, I had an enjoyable time. Maybe I'm learning the rules. Yes, things are changing. I feel at home now.

Students were now having more subtle insights about the changes in themselves and were seeing them in the context of their own culture:

> Had a continental dinner and I am aware that I am missing some things more than the missed things have to offer. Reminded me of my mechanized life back home. I am more respectful of Guamanian ways of life as I recall how so many people take time to talk with us, never seem in a hurry, and appear relaxed. I think I have been missing things that do not deserve so much missing.

> What is happening in me is exciting even though there are still times when I do not know how to behave.

> Now I see and enjoy the beauty, the people, and their way of living. I am still afraid of imposing on people so I hold back, afraid I will be a nuisance. People in the United States tend to be so busy doing things they don't want to be bothered and I can't quite get away from this feeling. I'm going to do less talking and more listening.

> Today I realize the relevance of culture in behavior. If one understands behavior in this sense, perhaps a different educational approach is needed in school. Maybe it takes a certain degree of severance from homeland to become truly bicultural.

Cultural observations in the journals now reflected an acceptance of differences and a clear search for an understanding of the new culture. For example, one student pulled together what had been said in the journals about fiestas and then talked with a number of Guamanians about their purpose, thinking to find a clue to something the group had not understood—the pattern of invitations.

By this point several students showed acceptance of the fact that differences in verbal and non-verbal communication were no longer simply matters for annoyance or frustration but were crucial to understand if they were to communicate with people of different cultures or ethnic or subcultural groups. This change from cognitive, passive understanding to affective, active acceptance was characteristic of this period.

Analysis of the journals during this period suggested that most of the students were moving through the twilight zone from feeling like outsiders to feeling like insiders, i.e., they were moving toward new perspectives, a new perception of Guamanian culture, and were feeling accepted by Guamanians.

The Field Seminar

In general, the field seminar sessions reflected acceptance of and a sense of stimulation from the cultural differences the students were experiencing. Most students were now very much involved in their relationships with Guamanians. Some of their comments relating to changes in themselves have an evaluative quality; the discussions about their cultural observations show an increasing ability to see connections among formerly discrete concepts. One student who had been struggling to identify with the Guamanian concept of sharing spoke of frustration:

> I was trying to share in the Guamanian way and didn't know what to do. I'm beginning to see the Guamanian way a little more clearly. I am caught in my individualistic ways and I don't know how to move. I am nervous about asking if I can help. In the United States people might be offended if I just pitch in. I think, here, I should just pitch in.

Later in the week the student wrote:

> Last week I thought I needed more interaction with people individually, but yesterday I saw it all in a different way. I am beginning to see how the rules work and I have some feeling of being accepted by the group. I feel much more a part of the people, even the children.

Several different ways of approaching cultural ideas emerged in the seminar sessions in this period. Recognizing differences between Guamanians and their own concepts of husband-wife relationships, the students examined what they understood about the Guamanian concept:

> What do we know about husband-wife relationships? How well does the couple know each other? What is the primary value in the relationship? The roles appear to be fairly clearly defined, and that may simplify things. The couple normally has known each other most of their lives, they usually come from the same village. In the United States emphasis is placed on companionship in marriage, but is this a priority value here? Is it a significant concept? Or is it as in "Fiddler on the Roof," when he asked his wife, "Do you love me?" and she responds, "What do you mean, do I love you?" Perhaps Guamanians assume that love exists and it is not necessary to talk about it.

A good deal of scattered, but recurring, discussion had occurred over the weeks about parent-youth relationships. Now students, noting that the chaperone system with respect to dating was a traditional practice, asked what beliefs had led to the use of this system. Did it involve a belief—which they thought was held in some cultures—that a man and woman alone together would inevitably have sex (actually, the belief is more complicated than that), and, if so, do they also associate dating with having sex? The students thought there was some evidence of this attitude among parents who hold to traditional practices and either forbid dating or permit it only with a chaperone. The attitude, furthermore, appears to have been transmitted to the youth who act accordingly. Some parents have moved away from the traditional beliefs and practices and permit dating under certain circumstances. Many parents know that a girl will tell them she is going somewhere and instead will meet a boy. The youth know the parents know what they are doing, but they find "ways to do some things they want to do without making waves at home." For some parents this may mean the youth are "out of control." Others see it as evidence of a transition that is taking place but may approach it either through punishment or by ignoring it. The point the students made is that discussion between parents and youth as a means of understanding their differences and arriving at some workable plan of action does not appear to be commonly used—as it might be in American culture.

One other approach used by the students to bring out an awareness of differences in values should be noted: they began challenging each other, using their own differing cultural perceptions and values to make their points. One student told of a situation where a teacher was holding a class at a Center and someone came in and started the juke box. The student saw this as a disturbance and was upset but concluded the teacher did not see it as such since she simply moved her class outside. Another student disagreed:

> I think the teacher did see it as a disturbance; she frowned momentarily and then took the children outside. We might conjecture that she turned a negative into a positive experience and thought why not have the children dance to the music.

The discussion shifted to the possible differences in the way Guamanians and statesiders might respond to the situation. One student felt the action was rude and insulting and would have spoken to the person or stopped the juke box by pulling out the plug. Another thought a Guamanian would not handle it by direct confrontation but would tend to look for an indirect solution and perhaps not take this kind of incident so personally since it happened in a public place.

These illustrations show some of the different ways by which students were trying to feel their way into Guamanian culture—trying to understand how Guamanians think, feel, and act, and the context in which they do so.

FOURTH STAGE: NEW PERSPECTIVES

Journals

One student wrote: "I'm still not taking enough chance, enough risks. When I tried today, it worked!" Some felt alien to their early thoughts and feelings: "For people who had so many negative frustrations at the beginning we have certainly come a long way." One student, among several who seemed to anticipate a possible re-entry shock, said: "Hawaii seems foreign. Even my parents seem like strangers. Makes me wonder what adjustments are to be made when we get home." A student who had experienced considerable early frustration said: "I am more comfortable with not knowing, not having answers, more willing to explore ideas and still not have answers."

Some students spoke of their perspectives in relation to the purpose of the project. For instance, one believed that the experience could be generalized to more than one culture; another was at last convinced about the value of culture-general rather than culture-specific learning; still another asked: "Is biculturality different from adjusting? I think it is. I think it is developing in yourself a new way of looking at things, at people, at the world."

During this period students began to identify new perspectives with regard to their own cultural values:

> I am beginning to look at my culture in perspective. Learning what other people do is making me look at what I do in comparison. That is a value in this culture learning. I am questioning values and things I have previously taken for granted. Is all our American individualism a good thing? It leads to a lot of lonely, left-out people. In the United States, initial acceptance is faster than in Guam but often there is no real feeling of closeness and trust as here. Generosity and thoughtfulness have, I think, higher value and are more prevalent here than in the U.S. People are less ego-centered. I could learn from them.

The Field Seminar

Some of the probing which appeared in the journals was carried into the seminar sessions and illustrated the degree to which students could feel and think as Guamanians. At the end of a session one student perceptively commented, "When you are in a culture you learn some of the inconsistencies in patterns, the reality that doesn't come through in a book."

In sum, the students' comments reflected a widening of perspectives and views about themselves, their own and the other culture, and a sense of confidence in their capacities to find their way through most situations. This is exactly what they have done.

The impact of the Guamanians on the students is clear. By virtue of the students' presence in Guam, they also had an impact on Guamanians. One example follows. Guamanian women are ordinarily reluctant to speak out in mixed gatherings. As one person said, "For a Guamanian woman, meeting a stranger is not an everyday occurrence." It calls for some changes in the normal way of doing things. However, the evening of the Parish Council party, their last "sharing with us," anyone who felt like saying something was invited to do so. A young woman who was close to some of the students and whom we all loved apologized a bit but then simply and beautifully told the group she had learned more about her own culture in the weeks of association with the students than she had known in her entire life. The spirit and the feeling she conveyed to all and the fact that she had dared to take the risk in speaking this way and sharing her experience with others was both touching and exciting.

It may be that the students did for some Guamanians just what the Guamanians did for us—helped them to become aware of their own cultural conditioning. This may, indeed, be one thing we can do for each other in cross-cultural learning.

OVERALL LEARNING

We present here a collection of comments by the American students made subsequent to the program which attempt to capture a critical aspect of their learning. In these comments the students reveal changes in themselves of considerable depth, especially in the achievement of new insights into their own culture and behavior, and in the attainment of greater comfort, enjoyment, and flexibility in interpersonal relationships and in dealing with unfamiliar situations. They also demonstrate growth in cross-cultural competence and ability to function more effectively in cross-cultural situations, particularly in communicating with people of other cultures or subcultures.

I am more tolerant of new and different ways of doing things . . . [the experience] has helped me to see the use of different solutions to a problem and made me stop to reconsider the various "answers" I had formulated in the past. This relates to another change I feel . . . I am not nearly so quick to express my viewpoint. I now feel the need to stop . . . and examine the issue involved. . . . I have become more tolerant of others with whom I disagree . . .

I am risking much more in meeting people and this has resulted in growth of more meaningful interpersonal relationships . . . I feel that culture learning becomes more and more meaningful with time. . . . It has given me freedom to look at and examine myself. . . . I am changed in my outlook and in what I can do, but others may not be able to notice it. I enjoy what I feel.

Now I really understand at gut level . . . that there are radical differences in life styles, not merely minor deviations from the way I live . . . This understanding and what I see now as an appreciation for differences has to alter some values and ought to permit me to accept people more on their terms than mine.

I became aware of the importance of metacommunication, that is, the meaning of a message is derived from the entire context within which it is given. I'm aware that we communicate more by voice tones, inflection, and a myriad of nonverbal cues than by actual words themselves. I'm also aware that different cultures operate with different cues. This can be confusing and lead to bad feeling on both sides. I'm now more likely to check out the meaning of a communication rather than respond with anger or withdrawal.

. . . culture is so all pervasive that it is difficult to encompass it in words. Culture to me is analogous to language. A person grows up with language all around him, and . . . learns to use it and it becomes a 'natural' part of himself. If he never hears another language . . . he will take what he says and how he says it for granted, never knowing that there are things he cannot say, sounds he cannot make, and thoughts he cannot think because they are outside of the structure of his language. However, when he becomes exposed to and learns a foreign language, he sees that there are other ways of saying things and other concepts that words can imply. He also becomes more aware of the structure and internal make-up of his own language through comparison and contrast with the foreign language. More importantly he becomes more aware of differentness. He becomes open not just to one other way but to the possibility of many other ways of saying things. Culture is like language in that learning another culture opens a person's mental set to the possibility of qualitatively different ways of looking at the world and to a greater understanding and insight into one's own. OLD CHINESE SAYING: Culture is the water in the bowl that gold fish swim in.

ADAPTING THE DESIGN TO EXISTING STUDY ABROAD C PROGRAMS

The design for cross-cultural learning offered in this book constitutes an integrated educational experience. Each segment is carefully constructed to reinforce and build upon the preceding ones. It takes students through a step-by-step process in which cross-cultural learning is facilitated by the specific conceptual framework provided, the procedures established for pursuing overseas experience, and the manner in which the learning is integrated afterward. To achieve maximum effectiveness, those who implement this program at their institutions should examine carefully deviations from the pattern presented here to ensure that changes and adaptations—the need for which may arise in many cases—are structured to be consistent with the basic design. In the authors' experience, experimental programs in which there were substantive differences in design were significantly weaker than those which followed this outline closely.

The authors recognize, however, that many institutions may not be able to implement the program as laid out here. Even more likely they may want to introduce systemic cross-cultural learning into more traditional, on-going study abroad programs. While some improvising will be needed and problems encountered, one can hardly argue against intensifying the cross-cultural learning experience of the large number of students who presently go abroad each year.

In structuring experiential cross-cultural learning into academic programs, credibility is a major issue. We believe that credibility is built into our design because the cognitive dimension is clearly defined, structured

95

in and linked inextricably with the experiential and because the learning can be measured.

Achieving credibility when attaching cross-cultural learning to study abroad programs which have other objectives may not be as easy. Yet it must be done relative to both students, on the one hand, and faculty and administrators on the other.

The students must perceive the cross-cultural learning objectives as being as important as other objectives. This means that the concepts must be presented in a rigorous and challenging manner (with the staff and/or instructors taking them as seriously as the students), that the field experience must be organized and managed with care and attention to detail, and that the post-field program not be slighted. It also means offering credit specifically for the cross-cultural learning.

Faculty and administrators too must be convinced of the intellectual and academic rigor of the program. Too often supporters of experiential cross-cultural learning expect faculty and administrators to accept fuzzy definitions of what it is and agree to give credit for something that cannot be measured. Offering credit to students simply for having been abroad is a dubious academic practice and, as we have shown here, unnecessary in the case of cross-cultural learning. One of the principal aims of this design is to lay out the cognitive framework for experiential cross-cultural learning and show how it and the experience itself can be made both integral and viable within the context of traditional academic structures—courses, credit, tests, intellectual content, etc.

PRE-DEPARTURE SEMINAR

There is no reason why the full pre-departure seminar proposed in this design could not be offered where the number of students is small or faculty resources are extensive. The alternative is a shorter orientation program condensing the cognitive input and laying the groundwork for the field experience.

The time spent by many study abroad directors on culture-specific information could be devoted to cross-cultural learning theory instead. Stewart and Bennett's *American Cultural Patterns* would probably be the best reading assignment, since cultural self-awareness is the critical first step in cross-cultural learning. The rest of the basic theory should be introduced at least in outline with one or two exercises, perhaps the perception test and/or "BaFa BaFa." Preparation should also be given in listening and observing and in how to record one's observations in the journal.

FIELD EXPERIENCE

The critical elements in the field experience are developing relationships with people of the host culture, keeping the journal, and discussing with the guidance of an instructor the experiences, thoughts, and feelings of the students. The main problem here will probably be in providing for the attachment to the program of an instructor with the skills needed to handle the field seminar effectively.

While many if not most traditional study abroad programs encompass formal study of language, culture and/or some other specific topic, they also inevitably include unstructured cross-cultural experience. This experience is particularly strong for those who live with families. While in the two-month overseas component called for in our design, the family living experience may in some cases inhibit learning because of the difficulty in getting out of the "guest role" during the relatively short term of the stay, a nine- or ten-month homestay is another matter. The field training could, in fact, be focused solely on the homestay experience.

POST-FIELD PROGRAM

Maintaining momentum for cross-cultural learning when it is only a part of another program may be more difficult than when it is the central focus. But the follow-up is important so that students have the opportunity to reinforce their learning, cultivate the personal growth dimensions, and avoid closure. As with the pre-departure seminar, the post-field program could be as long as proposed in this design. It could also be shorter, worked into the re-entry term without having to compete seriously with other courses. But the students must be given the chance to interpret and re-interpret the field experience in terms of the conceptual framework and to view the experience as a whole in perspective under the guidance of knowledgeable faculty. One interesting potential is combining students whose overseas experiences have been in different countries and cultures (or parts of a single country quite different from each other).

REFERENCES
AND BIBLIOGRAPHY

Adler, Peter S. "Culture Shock and the Cross-Cultural Learning Experience." In David S. Hoopes (ed.). *Reading in Intercultural Communication*, Vol. II. Pittsburgh: Regional Council for International Education, 1972.

―――― . "Beyond Cultural Identity: Reflections upon Cultural and Multi-cultural Man." In Richard W. Brislin (ed.). *Topics in Culture Learning*. Honolulu: Culture Learning Institute, East-West Center, 2, 1974.

Adorno, Theodor, Else Frenkel-Brunswik, Daniel J. Levinson, and R. Nevitt. *The Authoritarian Personality*. New York: Harper & Brothers, 1950.

Allport, G. W. and T. F. Pettigrew. "Cultural Influence on the Perception of Movement: The Trapezoidal Illusion Among the Zulus." *Journal of Abnormal and Social Psychology*, 1957, 55, (1), 104–113.

Attneave, Fred. "Multistability in Perception." *Scientific American*, 1971, 225 (6), 62–72.

Barnhurst, Kevin G. "The Lumpen Middle Class." *The American Scholar*, 1951, (3), 369–79.

Batchelder, Donald. "Training U.S. Students Going Abroad." In David S. Hoopes, Paul B. Pedersen and George W. Renwick (eds.). *Overview of Intercultural Education, Training and Research*. Vol. II: *Education and Training*. Washington D. C.: Society for Intercultural Education, Training and Research, 1978, 45–63.

_____ and Elizabeth Warner. *Beyond Experience: The Experiential Approach to Cross-Cultural Education*. Brattleboro, Vermont: The Experiment Press, 1977.

Bennett, Janet. "Transition Shock: Putting Culture Shock in Perspective." *International and Intercultural Communication Annual*, 1977, 4, 45–52.

Bochner, Stephen. "Cultural Diversity: Implications for Modernization and International Education." In Krishna Kumar (ed.). *Bonds without Bondage*. Honolulu: University Press of Hawaii, 1979.

Brislin, Richard W. (ed.). *Topics of Culture Learning*, Vols. 1–5, 1973–1977. Honolulu: Published by Culture Learning Institute, East-West Center.

_____ . *Culture Learning: Concepts, Applications, and Research*. Honolulu: University Press of Hawaii, 1977.

_____ . *Cross-Cultural Encounters: Face to Face Interaction*. New York: Pergamon Press, 1981.

_____ and Paul Pedersen. *Cross-Cultural Orientation Programs*. New York: Gardner Press Inc., 1976.

Brown, Roger W. "Language and Categories." In Jerome S. Bruner, J. J. Goodnow, and G. A. Austin (eds.). *A Study of Thinking*. New York: John Wiley. 1956.

_____ . *Words and Things*. New York: Free Press, 1958.

Bruner, Jerome S. "Social Psychology and Perception." In E. E. Maccoby, T. M. Newcomb, and E. L. Hartley (eds.). *Readings in Social Psychology*. New York: Holt, Rinehart & Winston, 3rd. ed., 1958.

_____ . *The Process of Education*. Cambridge: Harvard University Press, 1961.

_____ and J. J. Goodnow and G. A. Austin (eds.). *A Study of Thinking*. New York: John Wiley, 1956.

Casse, Pierre. *Training for the Cross-Cultural Mind*. Washington, D.C.: The Society for Intercultural Education, Training and Research, 1980.

Cohen, Gail A. (ed.). *Summer Study Abroad*. New York: Institute of International Education, 1979.

Cole, Michael and Sylvia Scribner. *Culture and Thought*. New York: John Wiley & Sons, Inc., 1974.

Combs, Arthur W. "Intelligence from a Perceptual Point of View." *Journal of Abnormal and Social Psychology*, 1952, 47, 662–73.

Condon, John C. and Mitsuko Saito. *Communicating across Cultures for What?* Tokyo: The Simul Press Inc., 1976.

Dabrowski, Kazimirz. *Positive Disintegration*. Boston: Little, Brown & Co., 1964.

Detweiler, Richard A. "Intercultural Interaction and the Categorization Process: A Conceptual Analysis and Behavioral Outcome." *International Journal of Intercultural Relations*, 1980, 14, (3/4), 275–93.

Fersh, Seymour. *Asia: Teaching about/Learning from*. New York: Teachers College Press, Columbia University, 1978.

Foa, Uriel G., and Martin M. Chemers. "The Significance of Role Behavior Differentiation for Cross-Cultural Interaction Training." *International Journal of Psychology*, 1967, 2, (1), 45–57.

Getzels, Jacob W. and Philip W. Jackson. *Creativity and Intelligence: Explorations with Gifted Students*. New York: John Wiley, 1962.

Gibson, Eleanor J. *Principles of Perceptual Learning and Development*. New York: Appleton-Century Crofts, 1969.

Gibson, James J. *The Senses Considered as Perceptual Systems*. Boston: Houghton Mifflin, 1966.

Gochenour, Theodore. "Is Experiential Learning Something Fundamentally Different?" In Donald Batchelder and Elizabeth Warner. *Beyond Experience*. Brattleboro, Vermont: The Experiment Press, 1977.

Gordon, Raymond L. *Living in Latin America*. Skokie, Illinois: National Textbook Co., 1974.

Gray, Audrey Ward. *International/Intercultural Education in Selected State Colleges and Universities: An Overview and Five Cases*. Washington, D.C.: American Association of State Colleges and Universities, 1977.

Guilford, J. Paul. *Personality*. New York: McGraw-Hill, 1959.

Guthrie, George M. "A Behavioral Analysis of Culture Learning." In Richard W. Brislin, Stephen Bochner, and Walter J. Lonner (eds.) *Cross-Cultural Perspectives on Learning*. Beverly Hills and New York: Sage and Wiley/Hasted, 1975.

Hall, Edward T. *The Silent Language*. New York: Fawcett World Library, 1959.

————. *The Hidden Dimension*. Garden City, New York: Doubleday, 1966.

————. *Beyond Culture*. New York: Anchor Press/Doubleday, 1976.

Hallowell, A. I. "Cultural Factors in the Structuralization of Perception." In Larry A. Samovar and R. E. Porter (eds.). *Intercultural Communication: A Reader*. Belmont, California: Wadsworth, 1972.

Hammer, Mitchell R., William B. Gudykunst, and Richard L. Wiseman. "Dimensions of Intercultural Effectiveness: An Exploratory Study." *International Journal of Intercultural Relations*, 1978, 2, (4), 382–92.

Harrison, Roger and Richard L. Hopkins. *The Design of Cross-Cultural Training.* Washington, D.C.: National Training Laboratories, NEA, 1966.

————. "The Design of Cross-Cultural Training: An Alternative to the University Model." *Journal of Applied Behavioral Science*, 1967, 3 (4), 431–60.

Herskovits, Melville J. *Cultural Relativism: Perspectives in Cultural Pluralism.* New York: Random House, 1972.

Hoopes, David S. (ed.). *Readings in Intercultural Communication*, Vol. II. Pittsburgh: Regional Council for International Education, 1972.

————. *Readings in Intercultural Communication*, Vol. III. Pittsburgh: Society for Intercultural Education, Training and Research, 1976.

————. "Intercultural Communication Concepts and Psychology of Intercultural Experiences." In Margaret D. Pusch (ed.). *Multicultural Education: A Cross-Cultural Training Approach.* Yarmouth, Maine: Intercultural Press, Inc., 1979.

———— and Gary L. Althen. "Culture and Communication in Intercultural Relations." In David S. Hoopes (ed.). *Readings in Intercultural Communication.* Vol. I. Pittsburgh: Regional Council for International Education. 1971.

———— , Paul B. Pedersen and George W. Renwick (eds.). *Overview of Intercultural Education, Training and Research.* Vol. I: Theory. Washington, D.C.: Society for Intercultural Education, Training and Research, 1977.

————. *Overview of Intercultural Education, Training and Research*, Vol. II: Education and Training. Washington, D.C.: Society for Intercultural Education, Training and Research, 1978.

————. *Overview of Intercultural Education, Training and Research*, Vol. III: Special Research Areas. Washington, D.C.: Society for Intercultural Education, Training and Research, 1978.

———— and Paul Ventura (eds.). *Intercultural Sourcebook: Cross-Cultural Training Methodologies.* Yarmouth, Maine: Intercultural Press, Inc., 1979.

Hudson, W. "Pictorial Depth Perception in Sub-Cultural Groups in Africa." *Journal of Social Psychology*, 1960, 52, 183–208.

Janeway, Anne. "The Experiential Approach to Cross-Cultural Education." In Donald Batchelder and Elizabeth Warner (eds.). *Beyond Experience.* Brattleboro, Vermont: The Experiment Press, 1977.

Jourard, S. M. "Growing Experience and the Experience of Growth." In Abe Arkoff (ed.). *Psychology and Personal Growth*. Boston: Allyn Bacon, 1975.

Keeton, Morris T. and Associates. *Experiential Learning*. San Francisco: Jossey-Bass Inc., 1976.

————— and Pamela J. Tate (eds.). *Learning By Experience—What, Why, How*. San Francisco: Jossey-Bass, Inc., 1978.

Kohls, L. Robert. *Developing Intercultural Awareness*. Washington, D.C.: SIETAR International, 1982.

—————. *Survival Kit for Overseas Living*. Yarmouth, Maine: Intercultural Press, Inc., rev. ed., 1984.

Kolb, David A. *Experiential Learning*. Englewood Cliffs, New Jersey: Prentice-Hall, Inc., 1984.

Kluckhohn, C. "The Gift of Tongues." In Larry A. Samovar and R. E. Porter (eds.). *Intercultural Communication: A Reader*. Belmont, California: Wadsworth, 1972.

Krathwol, David R., Benjamin S. Bloom, and Bertram B. Masia. *Taxonomy of Educational Objectives: The Classification of Educational Goals*. Handbook II: Affective Domain. New York: David McKay Co., Inc., 1965.

LaFrance, Marianne and Clara Mayo. "Cultural Aspects of Non-verbal Communications." *International Journal of Intercultural Relations*, 1978, 2, (1), 71–88.

Lambert, W. E., *et. al.* "Evaluation Reactions to Spoken Languages." *Journal of Abnormal and Social Psychology*, 1960, 60, 44–51.

Landis, Dan and Richard W. Brislin (eds.). *Handbook of Intercultural Training*. New York: Pergamon, 1983. Three volumes.

Larsen, Knud S. "Social Categorization and Attitude Change." *Journal of Social Psychology*, 1980, 111, 113–18.

Lederer, W. J. and Eugene Burdick. *The Ugly American*. New York: W. W. Norton & Co., Inc., 1958.

Leeper, R. "An Experiment with Ambiguous Figures." In D. E. Dulany, Jr., R. L. DeValois, D. C. Beardslee, and M. R. Winterbottom. *Contributions to Modern Psychology*. New York: Oxford University Press, 1963.

Lysgaard, Sverre. "Adjustment in a Foreign Society: Fulbright Grantees Visiting the United States." *International Social Science Bulletin*, 1955, VII, (1), 45–51.

Maslow, Abraham. "Defense and Growth." *Merrill-Palmer Quarterly*, 1956, 3, (1), 36–47.

Mitchell, Edgar D. "Outer Space to Inner Space: An Astronaut's Odyssey." *Saturday Review*, February 22, 1975.

Miner, Horace. "Body Ritual among the Nacirema." *American Anthropologist*, 1956, 38, (3), 503–07.

Murray, Gordon. "The Inner Side of Cross-Cultural Learning." In Donald Batchelder and Elizabeth Warner (eds.). *Beyond Experience*. Brattleboro, Vermont: The Experiment Press, 1977.

Narayan, R. K. *A Horse and Two Goats*. New York: The Viking Press, 1970.

Neff, Charles B. (ed.). *New Directions for Experiential Learning*. San Francisco, California: W. H. Freeman & Co., 1972.

Niyekawa-Howard, Agnes M. "Biculturality and Cognitive Growth: Theoretical Foundations for Basic and Applied Research." *Working Paper No. 1*. Honolulu: Culture Learning Center, East-West Center, 1970.

Ornstein, Robert E. *The Psychology of Consciousness*. San Francisco, California: W. H. Freeman & Co., 1972.

————. (ed.). *The Nature of Human Consciousness: A Book of Readings*. New York: Viking Press, 1973.

————. *The Mind Field: A Personal Essay*. New York: Viking Press, 1976.

Otto, H. A. "New Light on Human Potential." In Abe Arkoff (ed.). *Psychology and Personal Growth*. Boston: Allyn and Bacon, 1975.

Porter, R. E. "An Overview of Intercultural Communication." In Larry A. Samovar and R. E. Porter (eds.). *Intercultural Communication: A Reader*. Belmont, California: Wadsworth, 1972.

Pusch, Margaret D. (ed.). *Multicultural Education: A Cross-Cultural Training Approach*. Yarmouth, Maine: Intercultural Press, Inc., 1979.

Rhinesmith, Stephen H. and David S. Hoopes. "The Learning Process in an Intercultural Setting." In David S. Hoopes (ed.). *Readings in Intercultural Communication*, Vol. III. Pittsburgh: Regional Council for International Education, 1972.

Ruben, Brent D. "Human Communication and Cross-Cultural Effectiveness." *International and Intercultural Communication Annual*, 1977, 4, 95–105.

Samovar, Larry A. and Richard E. Porter (eds.). *Intercultural Communication: A Reader.* Belmont, California: Wadsworth Publishing Co., Inc., 1972.

Samovar, Larry A., Richard E. Porter, and Nemi C. Jain. *Understanding Intercultural Communication.* Belmont, California: Wadsworth Publishing Co., 1981.

Sanders, Irwin T. and Jennifer C. Ward. *Bridges to Understanding.* New York: McGraw-Hill, 1970.

Segall, M. H., D. T. Campbell, and M. J. Herskovits. *The Influence of Culture on Visual Perception.* Indianapolis: Bobbs-Merrill, 1966.

Sikkema, Mildred. "Cross-Cultural Learning: A New Dimension in Social Work Education." In Peter Hodge (ed.). *Culture and Social Work: Education and Practice in Southeast Asia.* Hong Kong: Heinemann Asia, 1980.

Singer, Marshall. "Culture: A Perceptual Approach." In Larry A. Samovar and R. E. Porter (eds.). *Intercultural Communication: A Reader.* Belmont, California: Wadsworth Publishing Co., 1976.

Smith, Alfred G. *Communication and Culture.* New York: Holt, Rinehart and Winston, 1966.

Steere, Douglas V. "Excerpts from 'The Spiritual Task of Teachers Today.'" In *Social Work Education and Development Newsletter.* Bangkok: ESCAP, no. 15, 1976.

Stewart, Edward C. and Milton Bennett. *American Cultural Patterns: A Cross-Cultural Perspective.* Yarmouth, Maine: Intercultural Press, Inc., 1987.

Tagiuri, Renato. "Person Perception." In G. Lindzey and E. Aronson (eds.). *The Handbook of Social Psychology,* 2nd ed. Reading, Massachusetts: Addison-Wesley, 1969.

Taylor, Harold. *The World As Teacher.* New York: Doubleday & Co., Inc., 1969.

Toffler, Alvin. *The Third Wave.* New York: William Morrow & Co., Inc., 1980.

Triandis, Harry C. "Culture Training Cognitive Complexity and Interpersonal Attitudes." In Richard W. Brislin, Stephen Bochner, and Walter J. Lonner (eds.). *Cross-Cultural Perspectives on Learning.* Beverly Hills and New York: Sage and Wiley/Halsted, 1975.

"The University Looks Abroad: Approaches to World Affairs in Six American Universities." A Report. *Education and World Affairs.* New York: Walker, 1965.

Wallace, John A. "The Educational Value of Experiential Education." In Donald Batchelder and Elizabeth Warner (eds.). *Beyond Experience.* Brattleboro, Vermont: The Experiment Press, 1977.

Wasilewski, Jacqueline H. and H. Ned Seelye. "Curriculum in Multicultural Education." In Margaret D. Pusch (ed.). *Multicultural Education: A Cross-Cultural Training Approach.* Yarmouth, Maine: Intercultural Press, Inc., 1979.

Wedge, Bryant. "Nationality and Social Perception." In Larry A. Samovar and Richard E. Porter (eds.). *Intercultural Communication: A Reader.* Belmont, California: Wadsworth, 1972.

Williamsen, Marvin and Cynthia Morehouse (eds.). *International/Intercultural Education in the Four-Year College: A Handbook on Strategies for Change.* New York: Learning Resources in International Studies, 1977.

Wofford, Harris. "The Future of the Peace Corps." *Annals of the American Academy of the Political and Social Sciences,* May 1960, 365, 129–45.